F O R E W O R D

I am delighted to write a foreword to "GOLF RULES - An easy guide" written by Margaret Smith who also gave us "From Tee to Green".

The Rules of Golf have always been very complex and complicated but I think over the last few years great strides have been made in an endeavour to simplify them so the game can be kept moving and played properly and fairly.

I would recommend this book to anyone, whether an old golfer or a new one - there is something in it to benefit all.

PETER ALLISS

ACKNOWLEDGMENTS

Firstly, my sincere thanks to Peter Alliss not only for the Foreword to this book but also for his continued support and interest.

Secondly, sincere thanks to Vern, my husband, and our family who, as with "From Tee to Green", have been a great source of encouragement, and to Roger Wood of "Design" for the diagrams and for designing the cover.

GOLF RULES

- An easy guide

CONTENTS

ABNORMAL GROUND CONDITIONS

Abnormal ground conditions are:
* casual water;
* ground under repair; and
* a burrowing animal hole, runway or cast.

You are allowed free relief from any of the above conditions (but **not** in a water/lateral water hazard) if your ball is in the condition or if the condition interferes with your swing or stance. Relief from interference with line of play is not allowed unless your ball is on the putting green.

A Committee may make a Local Rule denying stance relief in abnormal ground conditions.

You may clean your ball when taking relief from an abnormal ground condition.

To take relief:
Through the green: drop your ball within one club-length of the nearest point of relief (NPR), not in a hazard or on a putting green.

Bunker: drop your ball within one club-length of the NPR but both the NPR and the dropped ball must be in the bunker. If you are unable to get complete relief this way, i.e. the abnormal ground condition still interferes with your stance or your swing, you are then allowed to drop the ball as near as possible to the original position but not nearer the hole. Or you may take a penalty drop by:
-       implementing the GBL procedure (outside the bunker) for one penalty stroke, using as your reference point the spot where the ball originally lay in the bunker; or

---

- deeming your ball unplayable and taking a stroke-and-distance penalty.

Putting green: **Place** your ball in a new position (not nearer the hole or in a hazard) which will give you the nearest clear line to the hole. If this means your ball will now be on the apron of the green or in the semi-rough, you must still **place** the ball, i.e. you do not drop it just because it is off the surface of the putting green. The penalty for dropping instead of placing the ball is: Match Play - Loss of hole; Stroke Play - Two strokes.

When you are searching for your ball in an abnormal ground condition, you will not be penalised if it is accidentally moved; simply replace it, but, if you are taking relief, there is no need to replace it.

If, when taking relief from an abnormal ground condition, you drop the ball and it
- runs nearer the hole than the NPR;
- runs back into the condition;
- runs into a hazard, onto a putting green or out of bounds;
- runs more than two club-lengths from where the ball first struck the ground within the one club-length;
you must re-drop the ball. If it does not conform to the requirements on the re-drop, **place** the ball as near as possible to where it first struck the ground when it was re-dropped.

If your ball is lost or irretrievable in an abnormal ground condition, and you **must** have reasonable evidence that the ball entered the condition, substitute another ball, without penalty, using the point where the ball last entered the condition as the reference point for finding your nearest point of relief, and continue as shown above.

ADDRESSING the BALL

To address the ball, you ground your club and take up your stance, except that in a hazard you address the ball by taking up your stance only. You do not ground your club in a hazard whether it is a bunker full of sand or a water/lateral water hazard with or without water. Penalty: Match Play - Loss of hole; Stroke Play - Two strokes.

If, when addressing the ball by taking up your stance and grounding your club, the ball moves, you are deemed to have moved it - even if you step away from the ball and start again **without** grounding your club. Penalty: One stroke and the ball must be replaced before playing your next stroke or the penalty of one stroke is changed to: Match Play - Loss of hole; Stroke Play - Two strokes.

When your ball is in the rough or on a slope, it may be a good idea to take up your stance **without** grounding your club; that way you are not addressing the ball. Then, if the ball moves before you play the stroke, you will not be penalised because you haven't addressed the ball.

If, when addressing the ball on the tee it falls off the tee peg, you may re-tee the ball without penalty, but, if the ball falls off the tee peg as a result of a stroke, you count the stroke and then play the ball as it lies. (A stroke is the forward movement of the club - it does not include your backswing.)

When your ball lies just **outside** a bunker, you are allowed to ground your club in the bunker, but only lightly. Similarly, when your ball lies just **within** a bunker, you will not be penalised for grounding your club outside the bunker. These two points apply equally to a water/lateral water hazard.

To ground the club is to allow the ground or grass to take the weight of your club. To avoid grounding the club, support it yourself by holding it just above the ground.

If your ball comes to rest on an island of grass surrounded by a bunker, you are allowed to ground your club on the grass because it is not part of the hazard.

ADVICE and INFORMATION

Advice

During the stipulated round, you are allowed to give advice to, or take advice from, your partner and to take advice from either of your caddies but the penalty for asking for advice from, or giving advice to, your fellow competitor, opponent or anyone else in the competition is: Match Play - Loss of hole; Stroke Play - Two strokes.

Advice is:
-    suggesting to an opponent or a fellow competitor before he has played his stroke that he should use a particular club;
-    telling him that he is teeing his ball too high, too low or swinging his club too fast;
  i.e. influencing him in the playing of his stroke. However, suggesting that he takes a particular line of play is not giving advice except on the putting green.

For example:
Match play: If you ask your opponent for advice, you lose the hole. If he advises you as requested, he doesn't lose the hole since it was lost by you when you asked for the advice!

Stroke play: If you ask your fellow competitor for advice, you will be penalised two strokes and if the fellow competitor gives you the advice he, too, will be penalised two strokes.
            Say that your fellow competitor's ball has gone into a bush and because it is obvious that he is having difficulty in making up his mind whether to try and get the ball out or to deem the ball unplayable, you say to him: "I would deem the ball unplayable if I were you". Because you are

influencing that player on how to proceed, this does amount to giving him advice for which you are penalised two strokes.

Four-ball: In match play, if you ask one of the opponents for advice, you will be disqualified as far as that particular hole is concerned. If the opponent gives you the advice he, too, will be disqualified for that hole. In stroke play, if you ask a fellow competitor for advice, you will be penalised two strokes and if the fellow competitor gives you the advice he, too, will be penalised two strokes. These penalties do not apply to your respective partners.

If you and your playing partner are sharing a caddie, you will **not** be penalised if you ask the caddie which club your opposite number is using since you are allowed, at any time, to ask for and act upon advice given to you by your caddie.

Information

As far as the Rules are concerned, 'information' is best described, perhaps, as being relevant to the course. For example, you are allowed to tell your fellow competitor or opponent that the centre of the green is something like fifty yards from a particular tree or 'From this tee to that ridge is about two hundred yards', but if you add to this 'and I usually take my nine iron from here' you are then giving advice for which you will be penalised: Match Play - Loss of hole; Stroke Play - Two strokes.

You are allowed to ask your fellow competitor or opponent how far it is from a particular tree or shelter to the putting green as that comes under the classification of 'public knowledge' and is, 'information'. However, if you ask a fellow competitor or opponent how far he thinks your ball is to the putting green, you will be penalised: Match Play - Loss of hole; Stroke Play - Two strokes because that would be asking for 'advice'.

Information on the Rules and Local Rules may be given or taken, without penalty, at any time, but my advice to you is to be as knowledgeable as possible about the Rules of Golf without having to rely on your playing partner or marker to tell you what you may or may not do in a given situation.

Advice and Information

BALL in a TREE

If your ball is lodged in a tree:

When the ball is **visible** and **identifiable**, first tell your playing partner that you are going to proceed under the unplayable ball rule (one penalty stroke), then mark the spot on the ground which is immediately under the position of the ball in the tree and drop a ball within two club-lengths of this spot, not nearer the hole. If this is not a practical solution, you may take option (a) or (c) shown below.

When the ball is **visible** but is **not** identifiable, you may shake the tree to retrieve and identify it in order to proceed under the unplayable ball rule, but before doing so, you must inform your fellow competitor, opponent or marker of your intention. Otherwise, you may find yourself being penalised one stroke for illegally moving your ball and the ball would have to be replaced. Failure to replace the ball would change the penalty to: Match Play - Loss of hole; Stroke Play - Two strokes. If, however, the ball is not yours, your ball is lost and you must take a stroke-and-distance penalty.

Another option is to climb the tree and play the ball from where it lies, provided that the ball is not dislodged before you play your stroke or you will be penalised one stroke and the ball must be replaced. Failure to replace the ball changes the penalty to: Match Play - Loss of hole; Stroke Play -Two strokes.

To invoke the unplayable ball rule you have the following options:
(a)   take a stroke-and-distance penalty; or
(b)   drop a ball within two club-lengths of the spot on the

ground immediately under the position of the ball in the tree, not nearer the hole; or

(c)   go back as far as you like to a decent spot behind the tree and drop a ball on a line running from this chosen spot to the flag, keeping the point where the ball lay in the tree on this line.

NOTE 1   When invoking the unplayable ball rule you drop **A** ball (not necessarily the original ball) and the ball must be dropped - even on a putting green!

NOTE 2   Even if you can see what you think is your ball, if you are unable to identify it and it is irretrievable, the ball is 'lost' and you must take a stroke-and-distance penalty.

BUILDING a STANCE

If you build a stance to play your stroke, you will be penalised: Match Play - Loss of hole; Stroke Play - Two strokes.

When your ball is near the back edge of a steep-sided bunker, you may find it helpful to play the shot by putting one knee on the grass. If it is wet, it may be more comfortable to place your waterproof jacket under your knee, but, if you do, you will be penalised for building a stance. You will also have built a stance if you place a towel under your knees for the purpose of keeping your trousers clean when, for example, playing a difficult shot from under the low-lying branches of a tree. But, of course, there is no penalty for wearing your waterproof over-trousers!

After playing your ball into a tree, if it is sitting on a branch ten feet or so above the ground, don't be tempted to stand on a buggy or on the shoulders of your willing partner, or whoever, to play the ball as it lies or you will be penalised for 'building a stance'.

BUNKERS

A bunker extends vertically downwards but **not** upwards.

You have addressed the ball in a bunker when you have taken your stance.

Before playing your ball from a bunker, you must not ground your club or touch the sand on your backswing. Penalty: Match Play: Loss of hole; Stroke Play - Two strokes. However, there is no penalty for touching the sand as long as you are not testing the condition of the hazard or improving the lie of your ball if this is:
- to prevent falling or as a result of a fall
- to remove an obstruction
- to measure
- to probe for your ball
- to retrieve or lift your ball
- to place or replace your ball.

If your ball comes to rest on an 'island' of grass surrounded by a bunker, because the 'island' is not part of the bunker you are allowed to ground your club at address.

There is no penalty for placing a rake in the bunker before playing a stroke but, if this results in the ball moving, you will be penalised one stroke and the ball must be replaced. Failure to replace the ball changes the penalty of one stroke to: Match Play - Loss of hole; Stroke Play - Two strokes.

When your ball lies in a bunker, or has to be dropped/placed in a bunker, you may not touch or remove loose impediments, such as stones or leaves, etc., from the bunker before playing your stroke. Penalty: Match Play -

Loss of hole; Stroke Play - Two strokes. However, there is often a Local Rule allowing you to remove stones from bunkers and, **occasionally**, a Local Rule allowing you to remove leaves from a bunker.

You are allowed to remove movable obstructions, for example a sweet paper or the rake, before playing your stroke in a bunker. If the ball moves in the process, there is no penalty but the ball must be replaced. Penalty for not replacing the ball: Match Play - Loss of hole; Stroke Play - Two strokes.

When your ball lies in a bunker, if there is an immovable obstruction in the bunker as, for example a drainpipe, you will not be penalised if you touch the obstruction before making your stroke.

You are not allowed to lift your ball for identification in a bunker; if you do, you will be penalised one stroke. There is no penalty for playing a wrong ball from a bunker and neither do you count the stroke(s) in your score. If it is the wrong ball, replace it in the bunker in a similar lie as near as possible to its original position, not nearer the hole.

When your ball is 'hidden' in the bunker you will not be penalised for probing for your ball but if it moves, it must be replaced and the original lie of the ball recreated. So, if it was covered with the sand or leaves, etc., recover it. You are then allowed to remove only the minimum amount of covering to allow you to know where the ball is. You are not entitled to see the **top** of the ball, only to know its location. Penalty for infringement: Match Play - Loss of hole; Stroke Play - Two strokes.

If your ball remains in the bunker after attempting to play it out, you will not be penalised for raking the sand, provided that this does not improve your stance or lie of the ball for your next stroke.

Abnormal ground conditions

If your ball is in an abnormal ground condition (casual water, ground under repair or a burrowing animal hole, runway or cast) in a bunker or if the condition interferes with your swing or your stance you may lift and clean your ball, then find the nearest point of relief (NPR) and drop your ball in the bunker within one club-length of the NPR, not nearer the hole. If you are unable to get complete relief this way, i.e. the abnormal ground condition still interferes with your stance or swing, you are then allowed to drop the ball as near as possible to the original position. You also have the option of

- dropping your ball outside the bunker following the GBL procedure which is to drop your ball on an extension of an imaginary line drawn from the flag through the point where your ball was lying in the bunker, for one penalty stroke; or
- deeming the ball unplayable and taking a stroke-and-distance penalty.

If, when taking relief from an abnormal ground condition in a bunker, you drop the ball and it:
- runs back into the condition
- runs out of the bunker
- runs more than two club-lengths from where the ball first struck the ground within the one club-length
- comes to rest nearer the hole than the NPR
you **must** re-drop the ball. If the ball still does not comply, **place** the ball as near as possible to where it first struck the ground on the re-drop.

If your ball is lost or irretrievable in an abnormal ground condition in a bunker, drop a substituted ball in the bunker within one club-length of the point where the ball entered the abnormal ground condition, not nearer the hole, without penalty.

After playing your ball out of a bunker, use the rake and leave the surface of the sand as you would wish to find it.

CADDIES

You are allowed to be accompanied by as many caddies as you wish, but you may use one caddie only at any one time, otherwise you will be disqualified.

Usually, you are given free rein to choose your caddie but, beware, it might be a Condition of the Competition that a parent is not allowed to caddie for you, as is sometimes the case in Junior competitions; if it is and, for example, your father caddies for you, you will be penalised according to the penalty stated in the Conditions of the Competition - which might just be two strokes for every hole!!

If a caddie infringes a Rule, the player for whom the caddie is operating will be penalised according to that particular infringement.

When a caddie, who is shared by two or more players, infringes a Rule the player whose ball is involved is deemed to be responsible.

When you are asked to caddie for a player, you should be aware of what you may or may not do. For example, you may help the player by attending the flagstick; searching for his ball; repairing old hole plugs and pitch marks; removing loose impediments and movable obstructions; and cleaning his ball when he is allowed to do so under the Rules. You may also mark the player's ball but you may not lift it unless authorised to do so by the player.

You may place your player's clubs in a hazard, provided that this isn't done in order to test the condition of the hazard or improve the lie of the ball.

You may assist the player by standing behind the ball on or near an extension of his line of play/putt **but** you must move away before he plays the ball.

You may **not** drop a ball on behalf of the player; declare his ball unplayable; or lift a ball without the player's authorisation.

When your player's ball is on the putting green, you may not touch the line of putt prior to his stroke.

CARD

When playing on an unfamiliar course, take note of the Local Rules. They are usually to be found on the back of the score card as well as on the notice-boards.

It is your responsibility to ensure that your card shows your name, correct handicap, date, name of the competition, and the strokes allowed for the type of competition being played.

Failure to put your handicap on your card before returning it to the Committee will result in disqualification.

If you **knowingly** declare a handicap higher than that to which you are entitled and this affects the number of strokes received, you will be disqualified even if this doesn't come to light until after the competition has closed. However, if you declare a handicap lower than your correct one, you play off that lower handicap.

If you **mistakenly** play off a higher handicap than the true one, and it affects the allowance of strokes, if this is not discovered until after the competition has closed, you will not be disqualified. However, if you become aware of the error before the competition is closed, i.e. the announcement of the winner has been made, you will be disqualified.

If you are playing in a stroke play competition and the cards have been filled in and issued by the Committee, it is your responsibility to check that the details are correct, especially the handicap, before handing in your card. If the handicap is higher than it should be resulting in the stroke allowance being affected and not corrected before the competition is closed, you will be disqualified.

If you are disqualified from the handicap side of the competition for any of the aforesaid breaches of the rules, you will still be eligible for any Gross score Prize on offer.

As each hole is completed, check the score with your fellow competitor or marker before recording it.

At the end of the round, you should check the card to see that:
- the score for each hole is correct and settle, if necessary, any doubtful points with the Committee;
- your correct handicap is recorded;
- the marker has signed your card;
- you have countersigned the card;
and then hand it in to the Committee without delay.

Alterations to the individual hole scores should be made clearly so that there can be no dispute. Initialling alterations is not necessary under the Rules of Golf but does help to alleviate doubt.

Unless there are extenuating circumstances, failure on your part either to get the card signed by the marker or to countersign the card yourself will lead to disqualification.

You are responsible for making certain that the gross score recorded against each hole on your card is correct. If your recorded score for any hole is lower than it should be, you will be disqualified. This disqualification penalty applies - even after the competition has closed, unless it was for failing to include a penalty which you did not know you had incurred. If the recorded score is higher than the strokes taken, that score stands with no further action.

No alteration or addition may be made to your card once it has been handed in to the Committee, whether this means handing it to the relevant person or placing it in the required place, for example, 'the box'.

If your marker has to leave you after, say, six holes, necessitating the services of another marker for the remainder of the round, the first marker signs, if at all possible, to testify that the scores for the first six holes are correct and the second marker signs for the remaining holes. You then countersign the card to say that you agree with all the scores, as shown.

CARE of the COURSE

There are certain conventions to be observed where care of the course is concerned. Although the author is aware that care of the course is part of etiquette, she thought that the importance of the subject merited its own heading.

Try not to damage the course when taking a practice swing. Some Clubs prohibit practice swings on the tees, in which case you should see a notice to this effect on the first tee and/or in the Clubhouse.

Replace any divot made during play and really take the trouble to heel it in **but** do not replace a divot made on the tee; the reason for this is that you should be able to rely on the teeing ground being firm so that you may play your ball from a tee peg with confidence.

Leave the bunkers as you would wish to find them. More often than not, there will be a rake nearby, but, if there isn't, use a club or your foot to smooth the sand.

Observe the signs near the putting greens and bunkers indicating the correct route for you to take your trolley.

Repair your pitch-mark on the green either before you putt or before you leave the green. If everyone repaired just one pitch-mark on each green, the quality of the greens would be improved.

Do not lean on your putter when you are on the putting green or use your putter as a prop when taking the ball out of the hole.

Avoid damaging the hole when removing or replacing the flagstick or by using your putterhead to scoop the ball out of the hole.

You will not be penalised for disregarding the above conventions but you will be penalised for repairing a spike mark if there is any likelihood of it assisting you in the subsequent play of the hole. Penalty: Match Play - Loss of hole; Stroke Play - Two strokes.

CASUAL WATER

'Casual water' is water that is not a permanent feature of the course and is not in a water/lateral water hazard. There is no penalty for taking relief from casual water.

You do not get relief from casual water on your line of play except when your ball is on the putting green. For instance, if your ball is on the apron of the green and is free of casual water, you cannot get relief without penalty from casual water lying between your ball and the hole whether it be on the apron or on the putting green - and, if you mop it up, you will be penalised: Match Play - Loss of hole; Stroke Play - Two strokes.

Snow and natural ice may be treated as casual water or loose impediments but dew and frost are neither.

When your ball lies in casual water or the casual water interferes with your stroke or stance (except when a Local Rule denies stance relief) you may clean your ball and take relief, as follows:

Through the green: Find the nearest point of relief (NPR) and then measure and drop your ball within one club-length of the NPR.

Bunker. When your ball lies in casual water which part-fills a bunker, drop your ball in the bunker within one club-length of the NPR which must also be found in the bunker. If you are unable to get complete relief this way, i.e. the casual water still interferes with your stance or swing, you are then allowed to drop the ball as near as possible to the original position but not nearer the hole.

When your ball lies in a bunker which is full of casual water, you have the choice of:
- playing the ball as it lies; or of
- taking free relief by dropping the ball in the shallowest part of the water making sure that this is as near as possible to the original position of the ball but not nearer the hole.

You also have the option of
- playing the ball from outside the bunker by implementing the 'Go back as far as you like' (GBL) procedure for one penalty stroke by dropping your ball as far back as you like on an extension of a line drawn from the hole through the point where the ball lay when it was in the casual water in the bunker; or
- deeming your ball unplayable in the bunker, in which case you may elect to take a stroke-and-distance penalty.

Putting green: When your ball is in casual water on the putting green, lift the ball and **place** it at the nearest position which gives you a clear line to the hole. If this spot is on the apron of the green or in the semi-rough, you must still **place** the ball, i.e. you do not drop it because it is off the surface of the putting green. The penalty for dropping your ball instead of placing it is: Match Play - Loss of hole; Stroke Play - Two strokes.

When you have reasonable evidence that your ball is in casual water but it cannot be found or cannot be reached, you may substitute the ball. Also, when searching for your ball in casual water, if the ball is accidentally moved there is no penalty but if you intend to play it as it lies, you must replace the ball.

It is important to know that when you are in the process of taking relief, if the ball :
- runs back into the casual water
- runs nearer the hole than the NPR
- runs more than two club-lengths from where it first struck the ground within the one club-length
- runs into or out of a hazard
- runs onto a putting green
- runs out of bounds

you **must** re-drop the ball or you will be penalised: Match Play - Loss of hole; Stroke Play - Two strokes. If the ball does not conform to the requirements on the re-drop, **place** the ball as near as possible to where it first struck the ground on the re-drop.

When your ball is dropped, re-dropped or placed, if it 'stays put' for a second or two and then moves, the ball *must* be played as it lies or you will be penalised: Match Play: Loss of hole; Stroke Play - Two strokes.

CLEANING the BALL

Listed below are some instances when you may (or may **not**) clean your ball.

You may clean your ball:
- after marking it on the putting green
- after removing it from the wrong putting green
- after deeming it unplayable
- after taking relief from an obstruction or an abnormal ground condition
- when lifting it from an embedded lie
- when preferring its lie under a Local Rule
- when taking relief from a water/lateral water hazard.

You may **not** clean your ball:
- beyond the extent necessary to enable you to identify it
- when examining it for damage
- when lifting it because it is on another player's line or when it is interfering with another player's stroke - **except** that you are always allowed to clean your ball when it is **on** the putting green but don't make the mistake of thinking that the apron is part of the green!

If you clean your ball illegally, you will be penalised one stroke. However, if, at the same time, you incur a penalty for another reason, there is no additional penalty for cleaning the ball. For clarification:

Example 1
Your ball, which is nearer to the hole, and that of your fellow competitor/opponent are 6" apart in the same bunker. You mark and lift your ball but, while you are waiting for him to take his shot, you clean your ball. Penalty: One stroke for

illegally cleaning the ball.

Example 2
The situation is as above but, this time, you lift the ball without first marking its position. Penalty: One stroke for not marking the ball but no penalty incurred for cleaning the ball.

Example 3
Your ball has been played into a muddy area in the rough. Without involving your playing partner or marker, you mark and lift the ball in order to identify it and clean more of the ball than is necessary. Penalty: One stroke for not informing your fellow competitor, opponent or marker of your intention to mark and lift your ball but no additional penalty for cleaning the ball beyond the extent necessary to identify it.

CLUBS

The maximum number of clubs you are allowed to carry is fourteen.

When you start a stipulated round with a full compliment, you are limited to that selection except that if you damage a club in the normal course of play to the extent that it has become unfit for play, e.g. loosened clubhead or a broken shaft, you may replace that club with a club of your choice or have it repaired as long as you do not unduly delay play, the penalty for which is: Match Play - Loss of hole; Stroke Play - Two strokes.

If you damage a club other than in the normal course of play, you are not allowed to replace that club and if the damage has changed its playing characteristics, you are not allowed to use it. Penalty: Disqualification.

A club damaged in the normal course of play is one that is damaged whilst making a practice swing, making a stroke or playing a practice stroke.

When you start with fourteen clubs, you are not allowed to replace a lost club. See penalties shown below.

If you start with less than fourteen clubs, you may add further clubs to bring the number up to the maximum. You may add, or replace a club, by borrowing one provided that it had not been selected for play by another player on the course.

When you start with more than fourteen clubs, or make the discovery during the round, you will be penalised according to the penalties shown below. Once the discovery is made, you must declare the excess club out of play and you may not use it for the remainder of the round or you will be disqualified.

You will not be penalised for carrying your own clubs and those of your partner in one bag, provided that the clubs are clearly identifiable and that neither of you uses the other's clubs. Also, you and your partner may share a set of clubs, provided that the number of clubs does not exceed fourteen.

Penalties for breaching the Rules - as above
Match play: At the end of the hole on which the breach is discovered, the match is adjusted to take into account the deduction of one hole for each hole on which the breach occurred, up to a maximum of two holes per round.

Stroke play: Two strokes for each hole on which the breach occurred, up to a maximum of four strokes per round. For example, if two strokes are to be added to your score, they will go onto the score for the first hole breached and, if four strokes are to be added, two strokes will be added to each of the first and second holes breached.

Stableford: Two points to be deducted from the total score for the round for each hole on which the breach occurred, up to a maximum of four points per round.

NOTE   When you unduly delay play between holes, the penalty applies to the next hole, i.e. you are delaying play of the next hole.

COMPETITIONS

Bogey/Par

A bogey/par competition is played against the par for each hole on the course, i.e. you play a match against the course, but, unlike the course, you get your allotted number of strokes - unless you play off scratch.

How to Score
Example 1 - Par 3 hole (where you do not receive a stroke)
You halve the hole with a score of 3, win the hole with 2 strokes or less and lose the hole with a score of 4 strokes, but, taking 4 or more strokes is a waste of time because the result of the hole is settled!

Example 2 - Par 4 hole (on which you receive one stroke)
You halve the hole with 5 strokes (5 net 4), and win the hole with 4 net 3.

Example 3 - Par 5 hole (on which you receive two strokes)
You halve the hole with 7 strokes (7 net 5), win the hole with 6 or less strokes.

Example 4 - Par 4 hole (on which you receive one stroke)
You play four strokes but wrongly record 3 net 2, this **wins** the hole, but the correct score of 4 net 3 would also win the hole. Because the result of the hole was not affected there was no infringement of the rule and the result stands.

NOTE   As soon as the result of the hole is settled, it helps to keep play moving if you pick up your ball. Beware of slow play - **always** play without delay.

How to mark the card

For a win, show a plus sign (+); for a loss, show a minus sign (-); and for a half, show 0.

The winner of the competition is the competitor with the highest score. (Not necessarily the player who wins the most holes.) For example:

Player A	wins	6 holes	=	+6
	halves	8	=	0
	loses	4	=	-4
		Score:		+2

Player B	wins	5 holes	=	+5
	halves	11	=	0
	loses	2	=	-2
		Score:		+3

Four-ball better-ball

A side may consist of either one or two players, each side playing against the better-ball of the other side.

A side of one player may be increased to two players during the round but only at the **start** of a hole.

If a latecomer joins his partner **during** the playing of a hole, he may give him advice but, he is not allowed to play until the start of the next hole; if he does, he will be disqualified for that hole and if any of his strokes help his partner's play, or adversely affect either of the opponent's play, then his partner will also be disqualified for that hole.

The partnership may, at any time, make the order-of-play

decision which they deem most advantageous but, on the putting green, it would be unsporting if this entailed standing on an opponent's line.

Stroke play
For the purpose of keeping the scores, the marker for each group identifies the fellow competitors as Player A and Player B, and the player with the better net score for each hole gets his gross score recorded in the appropriate column, otherwise that couple is disqualified. Always check to see that your card has been properly marked **before** handing it in.

When a partner plays the wrong ball, he doesn't count the stroke(s), played with it. He has to find and play the right ball and then add two penalty strokes to his score for that hole. If he fails to find the original ball within five minutes, he must take a stroke-and-distance penalty, or alternatively, leave the playing and scoring of that particular hole to his partner.

Match play
A partner who plays a wrong ball, except from a hazard, is disqualified from playing out the remainder of that hole. The owner of the ball replaces it on the spot from which it was wrongly played but:
-      if it isn't possible to determine the actual spot on which the ball is to be placed, estimate it and drop the ball as near as possible to the original spot but, on the putting green, the ball is **placed** near the original spot - not dropped
-      if it isn't possible to replace with the original ball, a substitute may be used.

NOTE   There is no penalty for playing a wrong ball from a hazard.

If a player plays from the tee when the opponents have the honour, there is no penalty. However, the opponents may, before anyone else plays, request the player concerned to replay the stroke in the correct order.

Mixed Foursome

A mixed foursome competition consists of a man and a woman competing against another man and a woman, each partnership using only one ball. The men usually drive from the white markers, so don't forget to check this out before starting to play.

Partners must drive from alternate teeing grounds. In the absence of a ruling by the Committee, it is up to each partnership to decide which of them will tee off on the first hole, bearing in mind the advantages which may be gained from any handicap allowance and, usually, the man's greater driving length from the tee.

To play each hole, the partners play alternate strokes until the ball is holed. If one player, say the man, has an air shot, the lady plays the next stroke, and vice versa.

Penalty strokes **do not** affect the order of play. For example:

Man plays shot from the tee	1 stroke
Lady plays next shot and puts the ball into the water of a water hazard	1 stroke
Penalty for taking relief	1 stroke
Man plays the next shot	1 stroke

Playing out of turn

In stroke play, if the man played when it was the lady's turn, the lady replays the stroke from where the man played; but,

---

if it was his tee shot, she now plays from within the ladies' teeing ground and the ball may be teed. The side is penalised: Match Play - Loss of hole; Stroke Play - Two strokes and **correction** is as follows:

The error must be rectified before teeing off on the next hole, or, if the error occurred on the final hole, a declaration of intent to rectify must be made before leaving the putting green, otherwise the players will be disqualified. Strokes played out of turn are not counted in the score.

Playing from outside the teeing ground
In *match play* only, the opponents are allowed to ask you to replay the stroke from within the teeing ground, no penalty. If so, it is replayed before anyone else plays and the original stroke is not counted in the score.

In *stroke play*, the partner who plays from outside the teeing ground must replay the stroke from within it. The partnership incurs the penalty of two strokes and correction is carried out as shown under **correction** procedure above. The stroke played from outside the teeing ground and any subsequent strokes prior to correction are not counted in the score.

If **you** play from outside the teeing ground but, when it comes to rectifying the error, your partner replays the stroke instead of you, your side will be penalised four strokes: two strokes for playing from outside the teeing ground and two strokes for playing in the incorrect order. What is more, **you** must play again from the teeing ground before your side tees off on the next hole, or, if you are on the final hole of the round, make plain your intention to rectify before leaving the putting green, otherwise your side will be disqualified.

Tee shot may be out of bounds or lost

When the man, for example, plays from his teeing ground and it would seem that the ball may be out of bounds or lost (but not lost in a water/lateral water hazard) the lady plays a provisional ball from the men's tee and is allowed to tee the ball. If the original ball played by the man is neither lost nor out of bounds, the provisional ball is abandoned and the lady plays the next stroke for their side. But, if the original ball is either lost or out of bounds, the provisional ball (played by the lady) becomes the ball in play and the next stroke will be played by the man. For example:

Shot played out of bounds	1 stroke
Penalty	1 stroke
The lady's provisional ball becomes the ball in play	1 stroke

If you putt your ball and it finishes, perhaps, two or three inches from the edge of the hole, **you** do not tap it in to finish the hole, your partner does that!

Mixed Greensome

A mixed greensome is played in much the same way as a foursome, the only difference being that instead of taking alternate shots from the tee, both partners drive on every hole. The partnership then has the choice of drive for the ball in play and the other ball is abandoned. For example, if the man's drive is chosen, the lady plays the second stroke, the man the third, etc.

If both partners drive out of bounds, the principle of abandoning one of the balls still applies, so you now decide which of you is to replay the drive. If it is the man, he plays from within the ladies' teeing ground, because, in effect, you have chosen the lady's drive.

Stableford

The scoring of this competition is based on a points system for each hole played. Thus:

For a net score of one over par	1 point
For a net par	2 points
For a net birdie	3 points
For a net eagle	4 points
For a net albatross	5 points

Example - Par 5 hole (on which you receive one stroke)

For	7 strokes	(net 6)	1 point
	6	(net 5) net par	2 points
	5	(net 4) net birdie	3 points
	4	(net 3) net eagle	4 points
	3	(net 2) net albatross	5 points.

The winner is the player accumulating the highest number of points for the stipulated round.

Texas Scramble - another popular team game

This game is normally played in teams of four players, one of whom should be appointed Captain.

All the players drive from the tee. The Captain decides which is the best-placed drive and then all members of the team play their next shots from the position of the chosen drive. This is done by the other members of the team dropping or placing, whichever is appropriate to the Conditions of the Competition, within a prescribed distance of this position. This procedure is adopted every time the members of the team play their shots until a ball is holed, i.e. the position of the best shot is used by the other team members.

When a ball is selected on the green, a marker should be placed one putterhead-length away from the ball so that each member of the team is able to **place** his ball in exactly the same position. Just a word of warning, when the first team member putts, if he does not sink his putt he should not continue until he holes out, even if his second putt amounts to no more than a 'tap-in'. Once he has put his ball into the hole, the hole is finished and his score must count, thus not giving tho other members ot the team the chance to hole their first putt.

Thirty six-hole

A 36-hole competition is made up of two stipulated rounds.

In stroke play, it is necessary to fill in two cards, one for each of the rounds, and both must be signed and countersigned.

After completing the first round, and before commencing the second one, you are allowed to ask for advice from, and to give advice to, your fellow competitor or opponent. Whilst playing each of the rounds, the normal Rules apply: no advice should be asked for or given, or you will be penalised: Match Play - Loss of hole; Stroke Play - Two strokes.

Yellow Peril

This competition consists of four players in a team who are listed from 1 to 4 on the score card.

On the first hole, the first-named team member is asked to play a yellow ball and each of the other three members to play a white ball. The team score for each hole is that of the yellow ball plus the best two net scores out of the three white balls. On the second hole, the second player on the team-list plays the yellow ball, and so on in strict rotation. It should be noted that in a round of eighteen holes, the first two players play a yellow ball five times and the other two four times.

Yellowsome

This game is played in the same way as a Greensome except that the choice of drive is made by the opposition. Very vicious! Sometimes known as a 'Gruesome Greensome' and not one recommended for a harmonious atmosphere after the competition!

CONCESSIONS

A concession may be made in match play only. You may concede your opponent's putt and you may also concede a hole or a match **before** its conclusion.

*A concession may **not** be declined* For example:
In a four-ball match play competition, your ball is some twelve feet from the hole for three strokes and your partner's ball is about three feet from the hole for two strokes - on your line of putt. The opposition concedes your putt for a 4 in order to prevent your putt indicating the line to your partner. Because a concession may not be declined, you pick up your ball and hope that your partner holes out on his putt to win the hole.

*A concession may **not** be withdrawn* For example:
A man and a lady are playing a match. On the first hole, the man has just holed his putt for a 6. The lady now putts and her ball finishes about a foot from the pin for four strokes. He says: "O.K. That's good enough" and concedes the putt for a 5. The lady says "No, I must hole out", to which the man replies: "O.K., you putt it". She misses the putt but this was academic as she had won the hole when her opponent conceded the putt.

A concession is not valid after completion of the hole For example:
You and your opponent are on the 17th tee. The score is dormie 2 in his favour. His tee shot heads straight for the flag but your ball hits the bank on the left-hand side of the green and disappears from view.

When you and your opponent reach the side of the green,

his ball is sitting about a foot from the pin with no sign of yours. You both search in the rough ground where your ball appeared to come down but after, say, four minutes, rather than waste any more time, you concede the hole. He wins the match 3 and 1. (He was dormie 2 and, by gaining this further hole, the score in his favour becomes 3 and 1.)

Flushed with success, he goes onto the green, picks up his ball but then finds your ball in the hole. The score, much to his chagrin, is now adjusted to dormie 1 because you had already won the hole before you conceded it.

CONDITIONS of the COMPETITION

Committees are allowed to impose certain restrictions under the Conditions of the Competition and, if you ignore or infringe a condition, you will be penalised according to the penalty stated.

Match play: Before commencing your round, you are allowed to practise on the competition course on the day of the match unless prohibited by a condition of the competition.

Stroke play: Before commencing your round, neither practice on the course nor testing the surface of the greens is allowed unless you are permitted to do so under the Conditions of the Competition.

You must be prepared to start play at the time specified by the Committee or be disqualified. However, in exceptional circumstances, a Committee may waive this penalty or, under the Conditions of the Competition, modify the penalty to: Match Play - Loss of first hole; Stroke Play - Two strokes to be added to the first hole, provided that you are prepared to play within five minutes of the specified time.

You are allowed to choose your own caddie but it may be a condition of, for example, a junior competition, that you are not allowed to have a parent or relative caddie for you.

The penalty for unduly delaying play is: Match Play - Loss of hole; Stroke Play - Two strokes but, in order to minimise this problem, the Committee may in the Conditions of the Competition restrict the time allowed for playing a stipulated round, a hole or even a stroke, the modified penalty - in *stroke play* only - being one stroke for a first offence, two strokes for a second offence and disqualification for a further offence.

DAMAGED BALL

If you think that your ball has become damaged during play of the hole being played, you may mark, lift (but not clean the ball - except when the ball is on the putting green) and inspect it but you must first tell your fellow competitor, opponent or marker that you intend to do so and you must allow him to examine the ball. The penalty for not complying with all, or any part, of this procedure is one stroke. If it is agreed that:
- the ball is not damaged, replace (not drop) the original ball
- the ball is damaged, substitute the ball by placing it on the spot from which the other ball was lifted.

If your fellow competitor, opponent or marker does not agree that your ball has become damaged, he must make his feelings known to you before you put another ball into play. In which case, you then either accept his opinion and play on with what you thought was a damaged ball, or in:

Stroke play only: tell your playing partner or marker that you intend playing a second ball; record the score for both balls, and then put the matter before the Committee upon returning to the Clubhouse, unless you have the same score for each of the two balls; and in

Match play: draw on the opinion of a member of the Committee for a ruling. If a Committee member is not available, you may substitute another ball but you must retain the original ball in case your opponent demands a later inspection by the Committee. If they decide the ball was **not** damaged and therefore should not have been substituted, you lose the relevant hole and the match result

---

is adjusted accordingly. You also lose the hole if you are unable to produce the ball in question.

A ball may be inspected for damage at any time, i.e. there is no restriction even if your ball is lying in a hazard, but, you are not allowed to clean your ball at all when examining it for damage, except on the putting green.

If your ball breaks into pieces after playing it, you do not count the stroke. You replay it without penalty by dropping a ball as near as possible to the spot from where the original ball was played. If the original stroke was from the teeing ground, you are allowed to tee up the ball.

DISPUTES

Match play
Settling a dispute in match play should be settled before teeing off on the next hole or, if on the final hole, before either player leaves the putting green.

If a dispute cannot be resolved between you, you may call on an authorised member of the Committee to help sort it out, but, if there isn't one readily available, you should agree to come to a decision without further delay. If a player wishes to make a claim to the Committee, he should tell his opponent his intention before teeing off on the next hole or, if the dispute arises on the final hole of the round, before either leaves the putting green. The Committee will not consider a claim made later unless it concerns facts previously unknown to the claimant or the claimant had been given wrong information with regard to the opponent's handicap or his score for the hole in question.

Once the result of the match has been officially announced, no further claim will be considered unless it is found that the opponent deliberately gave wrong information to the claimant.

Stroke play
If, during a stroke play competition, you are in the situation whereby you are not sure about the correct procedure, you are allowed to play a 'second ball', but:
-      you should inform your fellow competitor or marker that you will invoke this Rule **before** playing the ball in play;
-      you should nominate with which ball you wish to score if the Rules allow;
and before returning your card, unless you score the same

with both balls, you must inform the Committee that you played a second ball and put the details before them or you will be disqualified from the competition.

Example
Your ball is lying immediately behind a direction post. Are you allowed to move the post before playing your stroke? You think that you are entitled to do so but your fellow competitor doesn't know, so you inform him that you will play the ball as it lies and then you intend to remove the post and drop and play a 'second ball' from where the first one lay. Further, because you feel certain that removal of the post is within your rights, you tell him that you wish the second ball to count for the score. You then hole out with both balls and your fellow competitor records both scores for that hole.

For the purpose of this example, the first ball scored a 4 and the second one a 6. Having finished the round **and** before completing (or signing) the score card, you tell the Committee that you invoked this Rule and, since your procedure with the post was correct they, in turn, accept the score for the second ball (a 6!).

NOTE 1   The reason for designating the ball you wish to score is in case both actions are correct, i.e. you are allowed to play the ball as it lies or remove the post.

NOTE 2   You **must** inform the Committee of your actions, unless the scores are the same for both balls, or you will be disqualified.

This example highlights how valuable a good knowledge of the Rules can be and how useful it is to have a copy of the Rules in your golf bag. Should your on-course deliberations over the Rules threaten to take up some time, do remember to wave through the golfers behind. Who knows, in the group following, there may even be a member of the Committee!

Once a competition is closed, no penalty may be imposed, changed or rescinded **except** that you will be disqualified, even after the competition is closed:

- If you agree to waive a Rule of Golf (in *stroke play*, all the players concerned will be disqualified and in *match play* both sides will be disqualified)
- if your card shows a handicap higher than it should and this affects your stroke allowance, **and** you were aware of this fact before the competition closed
- if you record a lower score for any hole than was actually taken unless it was because you incurred a penalty of which, before the competition closed, you were not aware.

A competition is closed when the result of a stroke play competition is officially announced or, in the case of a stroke play qualifying round followed by match play, when you tee off in your first match after the qualifying round.

DORMIE

The term 'dormie' is used in match play only.

A player is 'dormie' when he is as many holes up in a match as there are holes left to be played, e.g. a player who is dormie 2 is two holes up with two holes left to be played.

For instance, when you are dormie 2, your opponent has to win the next hole to stay in the match. If he does, you will be dormie 1. If he doesn't but halves it, you have won by 2 and 1: you are **two** holes up, you remain two holes up after halving the next hole, and there is still **one** hole unplayed.

DROPPING and PLACING the BALL

Whenever you are taking a 'free drop' or a 'penalty drop', you must stand erect and, with an outstretched arm, drop the ball from shoulder height. If you do not comply with this procedure you will be penalised one stroke. However, you will not be penalised if you correct the error before you play your stroke.

If, when you drop the ball, it touches you or your equipment, your partner or his equipment, or either of your caddies, before or after it strikes the ground, you re-drop the ball without penalty. When this happens, there is no limit to the number of times you re-drop the ball.

For a 'free' drop from casual water, ground under repair, a burrowing animal hole, runway or cast, or an immovable obstruction, you are entitled to drop your ball within one club-length of the nearest point of relief (NPR). The ball is in play if it runs up to, but no more than, a further two club-lengths from where it strikes the ground but **must** be re-dropped, without penalty, if it:
- runs back into the condition
- runs more than two club-lengths from where it first struck the ground
- runs nearer the hole than the NPR
- runs into a hazard, onto a putting green or out of bounds.

If the ball does not comply on the re-drop, **place** the ball where it first struck the ground on the re-drop.

If your ball is on the putting green and there is casual water between your ball and the hole, you may **place** the ball (not nearer the hole or in a hazard) at the nearest point on or off

---

the putting green which will give you a clear line to the hole. Remember, you may deem snow and ice to be casual water if it is to your advantage.

When lifting your ball under a Rule which requires it to be replaced, you must mark the position of the ball before lifting, otherwise you will be penalised one stroke. If, during marking/lifting/replacing, the ball/ball marker moves, you may replace it, without penalty.

When dropping a ball in a hazard, it must come to rest in that hazard, not nearer the hole.

When your ball at rest is moved or played by an outside agency, replace it on the original spot. If this spot is indeterminable:
through the green: **drop** the ball but not in a hazard or on a putting green;
in a hazard: **drop** the ball in the hazard; and
on the putting green: **place** the ball
as close as possible to where the original ball lay and if the ball is not immediately recoverable, substitute another ball but remember to tell your playing partner or marker the name and number of this ball.

If you drop or place a ball incorrectly, for example in a wrong place, you may, **before making a stroke** and without penalty, lift the ball in order to correct your error.

The penalty for placing instead of dropping a ball and vice versa is: Match Play - Loss of hole; Stroke Play - Two strokes.

If you should play your ball onto the wrong putting green,

you must lift and drop the ball within one club-length of the NPR which is the **nearest** spot off the green, not in a hazard or on another putting green and not nearer the hole.

NOTE   You may clean your ball when taking relief from a wrong putting green.

Where 'double greens' are concerned, careful scrutiny of the Local Rules is advisable.

DROPPING ZONE

A dropping zone, or ball drop as it is sometimes called, is a small area of ground placed either to the back of, or to the side of, for example, ground under repair or a water hazard. A Committee may introduce a dropping zone under the Local Rules when prohibiting play from such an area, in which case the requirement is to use the dropping zone, without penalty.

When using a dropping zone:
- although you may stand inside or outside the zone to drop your ball, the ball must be dropped inside it
- the ball is allowed to run up to, but no more than, two club-lengths from where it strikes the ground
- even if the ball runs (a) outside the Dropping Zone or (b) nearer the hole than its original position, it is in play and **must** not be re-dropped or you will be penalised: Match Play - Loss of hole; Stroke Play - Two strokes.

Although the ball has to be dropped in the dropping zone, it does not necessarily have to be played from within the zone.

ETIQUETTE

When your partner, fellow competitor or opponent is about to play a stroke, be quiet, be still, do not stand too close and remember, if you stand ahead of the ball, you may get hurt.

Practice swings on the tees are prohibited by some Clubs. Notice to this effect will probably be found on the first tee.

Take pride when replacing your divots. Heel them in, if necessary, but do **not** replace a divot made on the tee.

Always repair your pitch-mark on the putting green and any others you may see nearby. Repair spike marks after all the competitors in your group have completed the hole.

A match involved, for instance, in playing nine holes should give way to a match playing a full round.

A lone player has no standing on the course so, when you are playing alone, you are expected to give way to a match of any kind.

Always '**play without delay**' but, from a safety point of view, do not play until the group in front is out of range, otherwise hard hats will soon be the order of the day!

Although you are allowed five minutes in which to search for your ball, call the group behind through as soon as you realise that the search is going to be time consuming. This will help to keep play moving. Another way of speeding up play is to play a provisional ball if you think that your original ball might be difficult to find except that you are not allowed to play a provisional ball if your ball has gone into a water/lateral water hazard or has gone out of bounds.

'This way' signs around the bunkers and putting greens should be observed for the purpose of protecting the condition of the course.

Leave the bunkers as you would wish to find them.

GROUND under REPAIR

Ground under repair comes under the heading of Abnormal Ground Conditions so taking relief for GUR is the same as it is for casual water or for a burrowing animal hole, runway or cast. There is no 'free' relief for GUR (or for casual water or a burrowing animal hole, etc) in a water/lateral water hazard.

GUR is often marked by a painted line enclosing the designated area. As the line defining GUR is part of the condition, if your ball is **on** it then it is **in** it.

A pile of grass cuttings, hedge clippings, or any other material piled for removal by the greenkeepers, comes under the heading of GUR even if not marked as such. However, if this material has obviously been left to rot, the GUR Rule does not apply.

When your ball lies in GUR you may play it as it lies (unless prohibited by a Local Rule) or clean your ball and take free relief, without penalty, by first finding the nearest point of relief (NPR) outside the GUR where there is no interference with your stroke or stance (unless denied stance relief under a Local Rule) and then proceed as follows:

Through the green: drop your ball within one club-length of the NPR not nearer the hole, not in a hazard and not on a putting green.

Bunker: find the NPR in the bunker, then drop your ball in the bunker within one club-length of the NPR. If you are unable to get complete relief this way, you are then allowed to drop the ball in the bunker as near as possible to the original position of the ball, not nearer the hole.

You also have the option of dropping your ball outside the bunker by implementing the GBL procedure, i.e. dropping the ball on an extension of a line drawn mentally from the hole through the point where the ball lay when it was in the GUR for a penalty stroke or of deeming your ball unplayable and taking a stroke-and-distance penalty.

Putting green: Place the ball on a spot to give you the nearest clear line to the hole, but not nearer the hole. If this new position is on the apron or in the semi-rough, you must still place the ball, not 'drop' it.

When taking relief from GUR if, after your dropping your ball, it:
- rolls back into the ground under repair
- runs nearer the hole than the NPR
- runs more than two club-lengths from where it first struck the ground within the measured one club-length
- runs onto a putting green
- runs out of bounds

you **must** re-drop the ball or you will be penalised: Match Play - Loss of hole; Stroke Play - Two strokes; and if the ball still doesn't comply with the requirements, place the ball where it first struck the ground on the re-drop.

You may also take free relief from GUR even though your ball is outside the condition:
- if, when taking your proper stance, you find you have a foot touching the GUR; or
- if the GUR interferes with the area of your intended swing.

When your ball is lost as a result of it entering GUR, substitute the ball and take relief without penalty as follows:

---

(1) establish, or estimate, where the ball entered the GUR

(2) find the NPR from (1) and

(3) measure and drop your ball within one club-length of the NPR

but reasonable evidence must exist that the ball entered the ground under repair, otherwise you take a stroke-and-distance penalty.

The margin of GUR extends downwards but not upwards but anything growing inside the GUR is **in** the GUR. Therefore, if, for example, your ball is in a tree in the confines of the GUR, your ball is in the GUR and you are entitled to take free relief (unless prohibited under a Local Rule).

HANDICAPS

Match play

Prior to the start of a match, you and your opponent should declare handicaps and note where strokes are to be given or received. If the handicap declared is higher than it should be (and it affects the number of strokes given or received), that player will be disqualified, but, if the handicap declared is lower than it should be, that player plays off the lower handicap with no redress.

Stroke play

You are responsible for seeing that the correct handicap is on your card. If you submit a card to the Committee without your handicap, you will be disqualified. If you **knowingly** record your handicap as being higher than the correct one (and this affects the number of strokes you receive), you will be disqualified - even if the competition has closed. However, since you are being disqualified from the handicap side of the competition, your gross score is still eligible for any Best Gross prize being awarded. If you declare a handicap lower than that to which you are entitled, you play off that lower handicap.

IDENTIFYING the BALL

Although golf balls carry a number and a brand name of the maker, it is advisable to add your own personal identification mark on the ball. Some players use a series of dots; some use their initials.

You are allowed to identify your ball anywhere on the course except when it is in a hazard. If you lift your ball for identification when it is in a hazard, you will be penalised one stroke.

When you wish to identify your ball, other than in a hazard:
-    you must inform your playing partner or marker that you intend to identify the ball;
-    you must give that person the opportunity to watch you make the identification and replacement of the ball;
-    you must mark the position of the ball before touching it; and
-    you must not clean the ball more than is necessary to make the identification

or you will be penalised one stroke for any, or all, of these 'do's and dont's'.

If your ball is in a bunker and you are unable to identify it without touching it, play it out of the hazard and identify it immediately afterwards. If it is the wrong ball, there is no penalty, you do not count the stroke(s) and you replace the ball in the bunker in a similar lie and as near as possible to its original position, not nearer the hole. If this happens in a water/lateral water hazard, you replace the ball in the hazard in a similar lie as near as possible to its original position but not more than one club-length away, not nearer the hole.

When your ball is in long grass, touch only as much of the grass as is necessary to allow you to make an identification. You will be penalised if you make any improvements to the area in which you are making your swing, to your line of play or to the lie of the ball. Penalty: Match Play - Loss of hole; Stroke Play - Two strokes.

Identifying the Ball

INTEGRAL PART of the COURSE

Most golf courses have obstructions, such as wooden or stone shelters, roads or paths, from which relief, without penalty, is available unless designated by a Local Rule to be an integral part of the course.

When your ball is sitting in, on, or lying close to an integral part of the course, there is no free relief. You play the ball as it lies or deem the ball unplayable.

To invoke the Unplayable Ball rule:
- take a stroke-and-distance penalty; or
- take relief by dropping a ball within two club-lengths of where the ball lay, not nearer the hole, for a penalty stroke; or
- implement the 'Go back as far as you like' (GBL) procedure for a penalty stroke.

To implement the GBL procedure:
Go back as far as you like on an extension of an imaginary line running from the flag, through the point where your ball was positioned and drop your ball on this line.

LOCAL RULES

When visiting another Golf Club, it is important that you acquaint yourself with the Local Rules of that Club before commencing play. They are normally listed on the score card. However, new/amended Rules may be on display in the Clubhouse although they do not appear on the score card.

The penalty for not complying with a Local Rule is: Match Play - Loss of hole; Stroke Play - Two strokes.

A Local Rule may, for example:
- prohibit play from ground under repair
- prohibit play from an environmentally sensitive area defined as ground under repair, out of bounds or a water/lateral water hazard
- deny stance relief from ground under repair, casual water or a burrowing animal hole or runway
- allow the removal of stones from bunkers
- give relief from drainage marks, sprinkler heads, aerification holes
- give relief for an embedded ball in the rough
- deem all stakes (except boundary stakes) to be immovable obstructions
- allow you to prefer the lie of your ball.

When preferred lies are in operation (placing), you may prefer the lie of your ball on any closely-mown area through the green. You are usually allowed to move your ball up to a maximum of 6" but not nearer the hole. To do this, you may lift, clean and place the ball or move it with your clubhead, without lifting, but its new position must not be on a putting green or in a hazard. Once the ball has been placed, it is in play and any further placement will incur a one-stroke penalty and the ball must be replaced. If you do not replace the ball, the one-stroke penalty is changed to: Match Play - Loss of hole; Stroke Play - Two strokes.

NOTE   A closely-mown area through the green is wherever the grass has been cut to fairway height or less, so look out for this on paths which have been cut through the rough and even around the top and sides of the bunkers.

I cannot emphasise too strongly that you should look closely at the Local Rules before playing on an unfamiliar course, and, as the Local Rules at your own Club are, undoubtedly, revised from time to time, if you haven't looked at them for a while, there's no time like the present!

LOOSE IMPEDIMENTS

A loose impediment may be removed without penalty except when both your ball and the loose impediment lie in the same hazard.

Through the green, it is a good idea to clear the area of loose impediments before making a 'drop'.

A loose impediment is a natural object such as:
* a leaf, twig or branch of a tree;
* a piece of fruit;
* a stone, provided that it isn't solidly embedded;
* dung;
* a worm/an insect;
* a dead snake;
* a plug of compacted soil left after aerification work;
* snow and natural ice which may also be casual water at the option of the player.

NOTE 1 You will not be penalised if you remove an insect off your ball except when the ball is in the bunker.

NOTE 2 Dew and frost are neither loose impediments nor casual water and may not be removed from your line of play nor from behind or from either side of your ball unless this happens when addressing the ball, removing a loose impediment or when repairing a pitch mark or an old hole plug.

Sand and loose soil are loose impediments **only** when on the surface of the putting green. So beware, when your ball lies anywhere other than on a putting green, you must not remove sand or loose soil before making your stroke or you will be penalised: Match Play - Loss of hole; Stroke Play - Two strokes.

When your ball is at rest through the green if, before addressing the ball, the ball moves after either you or your partner (or either caddie) touches a loose impediment within one club-length of it, you are deemed to have moved the ball. Penalty: One stroke and the ball must be replaced. Failure to replace the ball changes the penalty to: Match Play - Loss of hole; Stroke Play - Two strokes.

When the ball is on the putting green, if the ball moves as a result of removing a loose impediment, there is no penalty but the ball must be replaced. Failure to replace the ball incurs the penalty: Match Play - Loss of hole; Stroke Play - Two strokes.

You will be penalised: Match Play - Loss of hole; Stroke Play - Two strokes if you breach any of the following:
-	when your ball is on the putting green, you may remove loose impediments from your line of putt by using only your hand or a club and without exerting any downward pressure on the green
-	while your fellow competitor or opponent's ball is in motion, you must not remove a loose impediment on his line of play
-	when both the ball and a loose impediment lie in the same hazard, you are not allowed to touch or remove the loose impediment before your stroke. However, the Local Rules often allow you to remove stones from bunkers.

LOST BALL

When your ball is lost, other than in a water/lateral water hazard, you must take a stroke-and-distance penalty. If that means going back to the tee, you are allowed to tee up the ball again.

When you think your ball may be lost, other than in a water hazard, to save time you may play a provisional ball. You must say that you intend playing a provisional ball and play it before you or your partner move(s) forward to look for the original ball.

When reasonable evidence exists that your ball is lost in a *water hazard* you may take a stroke-and-distance penalty or implement the 'Go back as far as you like' (GBL) procedure. For a *lateral water hazard*, you have the further option of dropping your ball either within two club-lengths of where the ball **last** crossed the margin of the hazard or on the opposite side of the hazard equidistant from the hole. (Diagram on page 120.) When the ball is dropped, it must not come to rest nearer the hole than where the original ball last crossed the margin of the hazard.

To implement the 'GBL' procedure, drop a ball as far back as you like, keeping the point where the ball last crossed the margin of the hazard between the flagstick and where you drop the ball.

Your ball is lost:
- if it is not found within five minutes after you (your partner or caddies) start searching for it
- if you play another ball without searching for the original one

-   if you play the provisional ball either from where you would expect to find the original ball or from a point nearer the hole.

NOTE   If, after **two** minutes of your search time, you find a ball which you believe to be yours and play it, only to discover that it isn't, you are allowed to continue looking for your ball for a further **three** minutes. The time taken in playing the wrong ball does not count in the search time.

I have been asked on more than one occasion whether a ball is lost once the player turns his back on it. The answer, very simply, is 'No'.

Example 1
Your tee shot ends up in thick undergrowth and, after searching for two minutes, to save time, you return to the tee for a stroke-and-distance penalty. You tee up another ball but, before making a stroke, your playing partner who had continued with the search calls to say that your ball has been found. Because it was found within five minutes and before you played a stroke at the teed ball, your original ball is in play.

Example 2
Your stroke from the fairway heads off into deep rough and after searching for a couple of minutes you return to where you played your last stroke for a stroke-and-distance penalty. You **drop** another ball but, before playing a stroke, someone finds the original ball. Unlike Example 1, you must now disregard the original ball (it's a 'lost' ball) because the **dropped ball** becomes the ball in play.

NOTE Once you have **dropped** a ball, it is in play but a teed ball is **not** in play until a stroke has been made at it.

You will not be penalised if you move your ball accidentally while searching for it but the ball must be replaced if you intend to play it as it lies. Penalty for not replacing the ball is: Match Play - Loss of hole: Stroke Play - Two strokes, but, if you are taking a 'free drop' or a 'penalty drop', there is no need to replace the ball. However, if you replace the ball and then take a drop, there is no penalty for having replaced it.

When reasonable evidence exists that your ball is lost in an abnormal ground condition which is **not** in a water/lateral water hazard, you may take relief outside the condition, without penalty, by establishing the nearest point of relief (NPR) from where the ball last entered the condition and drop another ball within one club-length of this point, not nearer the hole and not on a putting green or in a hazard. If the abnormal ground condition is in a bunker, find the NPR in the bunker and the ball must be dropped in and played from the bunker.

NOTE: An abnormal ground condition is casual water, ground under repair or a burrowing animal hole, runway or cast.

When reasonable evidence exists that your ball is lost in an immovable obstruction which is not in a water/lateral water hazard, you may take relief by establishing the NPR from where the ball entered the obstruction and drop your ball within one club-length of this point, not nearer the hole and not on a putting green or in a bunker. If, however, the obstruction is in a bunker, find the NPR in the bunker and drop your ball in and play it from the bunker.

When two competitors play in the opposite direction from adjacent fairways, the possibility exists that the two balls may come to rest near each other. If the balls have the identical brand name and number, unless at least one of the balls is marked with the player's personal identification mark, it may be impossible to establish which ball belongs to which player. If this is so, both balls are technically lost and the players concerned have no option but to take a stroke-and-distance penalty.

MARKING THE BALL

To mark your ball, place a coin, ball marker or similar small object immediately behind the ball, away from the hole, thus enabling you to replace the ball in its original position. There is no penalty if the ball or ball marker moves accidentally when marking/lifting/replacing - simply reposition it; but, replacing the ball an inch or two in front of the marker could lead to disqualification!

There are times when your fellow competitor, opponent or partner will ask you to mark your ball one or two putterhead-lengths away from where your ball is at rest. For one putterhead-length:
(1)　place a marker behind your ball and then lift the ball
(2)　place the toe (or the heel, depending upon which way you are moving the marker) of the putter blade against the marker
(3)　select a tree, post, or other point of alignment on the line on which the blade is pointing, to enable you, eventually, to replace the ball more accurately
(4)　move the marker to the heel/toe of the blade.

To measure two putterhead-lengths, replace the toe/heel of the putter against the marker, making sure that the blade is on the same point of alignment and put the marker down again at the heel/toe end of the putter. When replacing the ball, don't forget to reverse the process or you will be penalised: Match Play - Loss of hole; Stroke Play - Two strokes. However, provided that you become aware of the error before you putt, you may correct it, without penalty.

When your ball is on the putting green, it is wise to have any ball on, or near, your line of putt marked and lifted, particularly in stroke play, because striking another ball with your own ball will attract a penalty of two strokes.

Before putting, some players like to line up the wording on the ball with the hole. You must remember that prior to lifting, rotating or even touching the ball, you must first **mark** its position or you will be penalised one stroke.

MATCH PLAY

Match play consists of two sides competing against each other for each hole and the side who wins the most number of holes at the end of the match is the winner. After taking into account the handicap stroke allowance, you win a hole when your score is less than that of your opponent and halve a hole when your score is the same as your opponent.

Before the match starts, you and your opponent should exchange handicaps. If your opponent says, for example, that he plays off 19 instead of 18, and this makes a difference to the number of strokes given or received, once the match has started your opponent will be disqualified. If, however, he says 18 instead of 19, he plays off 18!

Because the Rules of Golf for match play differ in many respects from those of stroke play, a medal card marked while you are involved in match play is not acceptable and neither is the result of the match. You are not allowed to play match play and stroke play simultaneously.

If you incur a penalty, you should tell your opponent unless this is fairly obvious to him as, for instance, when taking a penalty drop.

When, during play of a hole, your opponent asks you how many strokes you have taken, make sure that you give the correct score because, if you don't, you will lose the hole, unless you correct the error **before** he plays his next stroke. Also, when giving the net score, make it quite clear by saying, for instance, 'I've played 3 net 2'.

If, after completion of a hole, your opponent says he won the hole with a 6 when, in fact, he halved it with a 7, if the score is not corrected before either side plays from the next tee or, if at the end of the match before you both leave the putting green of that hole, he will lose the hole. If the incident occurred on, say, the second hole and the proper score was not established until a few holes later, the state of the match is now adjusted to take this into account.

You are allowed to concede the **next putt** to your opponent but, when doing so, it will be both clear and courteous if you pick up the ball and hand it to him. This will avoid any confusion as to whether or not you conceded the putt. Your opponent may **not** decline the concession and neither may you withdraw it. Similarly, when you concede a **hole** or the **match**, your opponent is not allowed (or likely) to decline the concession and neither may you withdraw it.

If there is a dispute between you and your opponent and a member of the Committee is not available to arbitrate within a reasonable time, the match should continue without delay. Any intent by you to make a claim to the Committee must be made clear to your opponent before teeing off on the next hole or, if playing the last hole of the match, before either of you leave the putting green. A claim made after this will not be given consideration unless you had been given wrong information, i.e. a higher handicap which affected the stroke situation or the wrong number of strokes taken. However, once the match result has been announced, the Committee will not consider a claim unless it is established that the opponent knowingly gave wrong information.

If, due to your ignorance of the Rules, you fail to take into account the necessary penalty incurred for violating a Rule, your opponent may overlook it. However, if you and your opponent agree to waive a Rule of Golf, the penalty is disqualification for both of you - even if the competition has closed.

When your ball is accidentally deflected or stopped by your opponent, his caddie or equipment (other than when attending the flagstick), no penalty is incurred. You may play the ball as it lies or, before either of you play again, cancel your stroke and replay it. Therefore, if you are involved in a 'three-ball', whereby you will be playing two matches, one against each of the two opponents, you need to remember that:

-       in your match with the opponent who was involved, you have 'the option of playing the ball as it lies or of replaying the stroke before another stroke is played, but,

-       if you decide to replay the stroke, you will be playing two balls until the conclusion of the hole, and

-       in your match with the other opponent, you **must** play the ball as it lies, i.e. you do not have an option.

NEAREST POINT of RELIEF

The term 'nearest point of relief' (NPR) is used when taking relief without penalty from:
- casual water
- ground under repair
- a burrowing animal hole, runway or cast
- an immovable obstruction
- a wrong putting green

} abnormal ground conditions

and, once you have established the NPR, you drop your ball within one club-length of it, not nearer the hole, not on a putting green nor in a hazard.

To find the NPR:

Abnormal ground conditions
When your ball is in one of these 'conditions' find the NPR by assessing, with the appropriate club, the **nearest point** outside the condition, not nearer the hole, at which, if your ball was sitting on this spot, you would be able to play it without the condition interfering with your stance or your swing. Once you have established this **nearest point** you have found the NPR.

Immovable obstructions
When your ball is in or on an immovable obstruction or too near to an obstruction to play it, assess, with the appropriate club, the **nearest point** outside the obstruction, not nearer the hole, at which if your ball was sitting on this spot you would be able to play it without interference from the obstruction. Once you have established this **nearest point**, you have found the NPR.

Wrong putting green

When your ball is on the wrong putting green, you **must** lift and drop it within one club-length of the NPR.

To establish the NPR find the **nearest point** off the green, not nearer the hole, where your ball would be clear of the green - that point is your NPR.   You do not take into consideration your stance and swing.

OBSTRUCTIONS

An obstruction is anything artificial, but excludes all items marking out of bounds, for example, fences, walls and stakes.

The Committee may declare a construction to be an integral part of the course, for example, a road or a shelter.

Movable obstructions
A 'movable' obstruction is one that moves easily for example, an abandoned ball. If, before playing your ball from a bunker you remove a sweet paper or a rake, there is no penalty because both are movable obstructions. A greenkeeper's tractor is a movable obstruction provided that the driver and/or keys are available without unduly delaying play; if not, it is an immovable obstruction.

When the ball lies in or on the obstruction, you may lift and clean the ball and remove the obstruction without penalty, then **drop** the ball (through the green or in a hazard) or place the ball (on a putting green) as near as possible to the spot on the ground directly under the position of the ball when it came to rest in or on the obstruction.

When the obstruction interferes with your swing, stance or line of play, you may remove the obstruction without penalty and, if the ball moves, replace the ball. Failure to replace the ball incurs the penalty: Match Play - Loss of hole; Stroke Play - Two strokes.

Once your ball is in motion, an obstruction that might have an effect on the ball must not be removed except for an attended flagstick or equipment belonging to the players in your group. The player who wrongly removes the obstruction is penalised: Match Play - Loss of hole; Stroke Play - Two strokes.

In order to save time, you may use a substitute ball if the original ball is not easily recoverable from the obstruction.

Immovable obstructions
A construction, such as a built-in water sprinkler; a greenkeepers' hut; and roads or paths that have been artificially surfaced, are immovable obstructions provided that they have not been declared by the Committee to be integral parts of the course. An artificially surfaced road or path is one that has been covered with wood chippings, concrete, gravel, etc., something that has been manufactured. However, if you come across some steps which are cut out of the ground and have not been artificially covered these steps are, therefore, an integral part of the course offering no free relief.

If your ball is up against a shelter, don't take it for granted that this is an immovable obstruction from which you may take free relief because it isn't always and the same goes for the roads and paths that run along some of our fairways. Under the Local Rules, you may find that these 'constructions' are not 'obstructions' they are 'integral parts of the course' which means that you are not allowed free relief from them.

There is no free relief from an immovable obstruction in a water/lateral water hazard. Anywhere else on the course, if an obstruction interferes with your stroke or stance, you may clean your ball and take relief without penalty as follows:

through the green: find the nearest point of relief (NPR) and drop your ball within one club-length of that point, not nearer the hole, not on a putting green nor in a hazard.

bunker: find the NPR in the bunker, lift and drop the ball in the bunker within one club-length of the NPR, not nearer the hole or on a putting green.

putting green: lift and **place** the ball at the nearest spot to give you a clear line to the hole, not nearer the hole and not in a hazard. Even if this new spot is off the surface of the putting green, you must place the ball.

If the ball is not easily recoverable or if reasonable evidence exists that your ball is lost in an immovable obstruction, you may substitute the ball and take relief from where the ball entered the obstruction.

You are not allowed free relief from an immovable obstruction which affects your line of play unless your ball is on the putting green and the line of putt is affected.

If your ball comes to rest on a bridge which is **not** over a water/lateral water hazard, you may play the ball as it lies or drop your ball, without penalty, within one club-length of the point directly under the position of the ball when it was on the bridge. The last option is not available if the bridge has been declared to be an integral part of the course.

A Committee may make a Local Rule to change the status of a movable obstruction to an immovable obstruction.

OUT of BOUNDS

Your ball is out of bounds
- when **all** of the ball lies out of bounds
- when your ball is on a line defining out of bounds - because the line itself is out of bounds

If the Local Rule states that the boundary of the course is defined by a fence, because (a) a ball is out of bounds when **all** of it lies out of bounds and (b) the boundary line is the nearest inside edge of the uprights, excluding any angled supports, the ball, as shown in the diagram, is still in bounds.

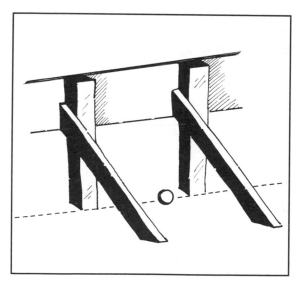

Because the angled supports are inside the out of bounds fence, they are immovable obstructions from which you may take free relief if they interfere with your stance or intended line of swing.

Where hedges and walls are concerned, clarification of the boundary line rests with the local Committee and should be expressed in the Local Rules. More often than not, however, a ball is out of bounds when it has gone beyond the course edge of the boundary.

If your stance, area of intended swing or line of play is impeded by any object defining out of bounds, you are **not** entitled to relief without penalty. You play the ball as it lies or deem the ball unplayable.

When a boundary stake interferes with your stroke, you will be penalised if you remove it, even if you replace it before playing your stroke. Penalty: Match Play - Loss of hole; Stroke Play - Two strokes.

When your ball is near a closed gate in a boundary fence, you must leave it closed even though it may interfere with your stroke. Penalty for altering the position of the gate is: Match Play - Loss of hole; Stroke Play - Two strokes. If the gate is open, however, you are allowed either to leave it open or to close it before playing your stroke. You are not allowed to move it to any other position.

When your ball comes to rest out of bounds, you have no alternative but to take a stroke-and-distance penalty.

If you play your ball when it is out of bounds, in match play you lose the hole. In stroke play, you will be penalised two strokes and you must take a stroke-and-distance penalty (three penalty strokes in all) to rectify the error. The error must be rectified before teeing off on the next hole or, if on the last hole of the round, you must declare an intent to rectify before leaving the putting green or you will be disqualified.

You may stand out of bounds to play a ball which is in bounds.

When your ball goes into a stream which is in bounds, if the flow of the water carries the ball out of bounds, you have no alternative but to take a stroke-and-distance penalty.

If you play your ball into a stream which is out of bounds and the flow of the water brings it back into bounds, the ball is **in** bounds. If the ball is now in a *water hazard*, you may:
(a)   play the ball as it lies;
(b)   implement the 'Go back as far as you like' (GBL) procedure;
(c)   take a stroke-and-distance penalty.

To implement the GBL procedure, the reference point you keep between the hole and where you drop the ball is where the ball re-entered the course at the boundary line. If, due to the nature of the course, you find it impossible to drop behind the hazard on a line from the hole through this reference point, you are allowed to treat the water hazard as a lateral water hazard and take a two club-length penalty drop on either side of the hazard, equidistant from the hole. Diagram on page 120. The ball when dropped must not come to rest nearer the hole.

NOTE   A Committee may make a Local Rule prohibiting play from an environmentally-sensitive area defined as out of bounds, leaving you with no option but to take a stroke-and-distance penalty.

OUTSIDE AGENCIES

Listed below are some outside agencies:
* a marker
* a referee
* an observer
* a forecaddie (ball spotter)
* a spectator
* a dog/cat/bird

NOTE Wind and water are **not** outside agencies.

In *stroke play* - all the competitors are outside agencies to each other. In foursomes and four-balls all partnerships are outside agencies to each other.

In *match play* - your opponent is not an outside agency to you and neither are you to him because you are both part of the same match. Similarly, in foursomes and four-balls you and your partner are not outside agencies to your opponents - but the members of your group are outside agencies to all the other players on the course, and vice versa.

When your ball at rest is moved by an outside agency, there is no penalty, but the ball must be replaced. In the event of the ball disappearing, provided that reasonable evidence exists that your ball was taken by an outside agency, **place** a substitute ball on the original spot. If this spot is indeterminable, you must **drop** a ball as near as possible to the original position, except that on the putting green the ball is **placed**, not dropped. Without reasonable evidence to the contrary, your ball is lost and you must take a stroke-and distance penalty.

When your ball in motion is deflected or stopped by an outside agency, you get no free relief. Therefore, if it comes to rest out of bounds, you must take a stroke-and-distance penalty.

When your ball is played from the putting green, if it is stopped, deflected or comes to rest in or on a moving or animate outside agency (except a worm or an insect), you must replay your stroke, without penalty.

When your ball is played from anywhere other than the putting green, if the ball comes to rest in or on a moving or animate outside agency, **drop** the ball as near as possible to the spot where the outside agency was when your ball came to rest in or on it. However, if this spot was on the putting green, the ball is placed, not dropped.

If, under any of these circumstances, your ball is not immediately recoverable, you may substitute another ball.

PENALTIES and PROCEDURES

'Go back as far as you like '(GBL) procedure
The penalty for implementing the GBL procedure is one stroke.

To implement the procedure when, for example, your ball is under a clump of heather, draw an imaginary line direct from the hole to a spot on which you wish to drop the ball, keeping the position of where the ball lay (the reference point) between these two points. Remember, the reference point is where the ball lay and **not** the general area of the heather.

When your ball has gone into a water/lateral water hazard, your reference point is where the ball **last** crossed the margin of the water hazard, i.e. not where the ball came to rest in the hazard.

If your ball crosses a water/lateral water hazard twice in one shot, i.e. the ball crosses the hazard and then rolls or falls back into the hazard, your reference point is where the ball **last** crossed the margin of the hazard. Diagram on page 122.

Nearest point of relief (NPR)
When your ball is in, for example, casual water through the green, the NPR is the nearest point outside the casual water where interference from the condition no longer exists with your ball, your stance or your swing. This must not be nearer the hole, on a putting green or in a hazard. When your ball is on the putting green, the NPR is the nearest spot to give you a clear line to the hole and when your ball is in a bunker, the NPR must be in the bunker.

If your ball lies close to, in or on an immovable obstruction, find the nearest point of relief as for casual water.

NOTE You are not allowed relief without penalty from an immovable obstruction in a water/lateral water hazard.

One club-length or two?

Do you have difficulty in remembering whether you measure one club-length or two for a given situation? You may find this simple adage useful: 'One club-length is free; two club-lengths you pay for'. However, in certain circumstances, some Clubs allow you to drop your ball without penalty within two club-lengths, or even more, but this will be included in the Local Rules.

Stroke-and-distance penalty

When your ball is lost or is out of bounds, other than in a water/lateral water hazard, you have no alternative but to take a stroke-and-distance penalty which you do by playing your next stroke from where you played the last one and adding a penalty stroke to your score.

If you played the last stroke from *the tee,* you must play the next stroke from within the teeing ground and you are allowed to tee up the ball again; *through the green* and in a *bunker*, drop the ball on or as near as possible to the previous position which, if not determinable, you estimate; and on the *putting green,* you **place** the ball on the original or estimated spot.

Beware!

Striking the ball more than once. This doesn't happen very often but could well happen, for instance, when you are confronted with a steep-faced bunker, or the like. Penalty: One stroke. It is sometimes called a 'conscience penalty' because the chances are you'll be the only person to be aware of the violation!

Before you make a stroke, your partner or caddie may stand behind the ball on or near an extension of your line of play or your line of putt but must move away before you strike the ball.

Waiving the Disqualification penalty
Only a Committee, as a whole, may waive, impose or modify a penalty of Disqualification; neither a referee nor an individual member of the Committee may take such action.

PRACTICE

In *match play,* you will not be penalised if you practise on the course on the same day as the match.

In *stroke play*, you will be disqualified if you practise on the course or even test the surface of the greens **before** the competition starts, or, if the competition is being held over two or more days, between each of the rounds. However, there is no penalty if you practise putt or chip on or near the first teeing ground.

When playing a competition round, you will be penalised: Match Play - Loss of hole; Stroke Play - Two strokes if you play a practice stroke - except that, between holes, you may practise putt or chip on or near the putting green of the hole last played or on or near the teeing ground of the next hole to be played but not from a hazard and without unduly delaying play. However, once the result of the hole has been decided, any further strokes played on that hole are not considered to be practice strokes.

The Committee may, under the Conditions of the Competition:
- allow practice prior to a stroke play competition
- prohibit practice prior to a match play competition
- prohibit practice on the green last played.

PREFERRED LIES

During the winter, or for other adverse conditions, some Clubs bring in a Local Rule which usually allows you to 'prefer' the lie of your ball on any closely-mown area through the green by moving it up to 6" not nearer the hole. To do this you may lift, clean and place or move the ball without lifting. Once the ball has been 'preferred', **it is back in play** and any further placement will incur a one stroke penalty and the ball must be replaced. If you do not replace the ball, the one stroke penalty is changed to: Match Play - Loss of hole; Stroke Play - Two strokes.

A closely-mown area through the green is where the grass has been cut to fairway height or less, for example, on the fairway, on the paths running through the semi-rough and often around the top and sides of the bunkers.

PROVISIONAL BALL

When you think that your ball might be out of bounds or lost, other than in a water hazard, to save time you may play a provisional ball. But, you **must** first inform your fellow competitor, opponent or marker that you intend to play a provisional ball and you **must** be quite specific about it, for example, don't just say 'I'll take another one'; you must say that you will be playing a provisional ball. Also, you must play it before you or your partner move(s) forward to look for the original ball. Failure to comply with these requirements will mean that this ball now becomes the ball in play under a stroke-and-distance penalty.

On the *teeing ground,* you play the provisional ball after your fellow competitor or opponent has played his first stroke and you may tee up the ball and play it from anywhere within the teeing ground; *through the green,* you drop the ball as near as possible to the spot from which you played the original ball.

You are allowed to play the provisional ball up to the point where you think the original ball is likely to be. If you play the provisional ball from this point or a point nearer the hole, the provisional ball then becomes the ball in play under penalty of stroke-and-distance.

If the original ball is found within five minutes, the provisional ball must be abandoned or you will be penalised for playing the wrong ball. Penalty: Match Play - Loss of hole; Stroke Play - Two strokes.

If your ball is lost or out of bounds, your provisional ball becomes the ball in play and you incur a stroke-and-distance penalty.

If you play your original ball into trouble and play a provisional ball which lands close to the pin, you may play it without searching for the original ball. But, if the original ball is found within five minutes and before you make another stroke at the provisional ball, it must be identified and if yours, played, and the provisional ball abandoned.

If your provisional ball Is holed from the tee, you don't have to search for the original ball but your fellow competitor or opponent has five minutes in which to search for it. However, if you pick the ball out of the hole before the original ball is found in bounds, the provisional ball becomes the ball in play under penalty of stroke-and-distance and your score for the hole is three strokes.

When you **know** that your ball has entered a water/lateral water hazard, you are not allowed to play a provisional ball but, if there is any doubt, you may play a provisional ball. If you fail to find the original ball within five minutes, play on with the provisional ball, but, if the original one is in the hazard, you must pick up the provisional ball and continue as if you had not played it.

PUTTING GREEN

If any part of your ball is touching the putting green, your ball is on it.

Your ball is holed when it is at rest inside the hole and all of it is below the level of the lip of the hole.

You must not touch the rim of the hole prior to making your putt unless it is to repair a hole the dimensions of which have become materially changed **and** there is no Committee member available to repair it for you. Penalty: Match Play - Loss of hole; Stroke Play - Two strokes. If there is an irregularity there, the careful player will repair it after all the players on the putting green have putted out.

You are not allowed to test the surface of the putting green by rolling a ball along it. Penalty: Match Play - Loss of hole; Stroke Play - Two strokes.

Whether your ball is on or off the putting green, you may repair a pitch-mark or an old hole plug on your line of putt and if the ball or marker is accidentally moved, replace it without penalty.

You are not allowed to repair spike marks, or to eliminate them by walking over the area, if such action is likely to assist you in the subsequent play of the hole. Penalty: Match Play - Loss of hole; Stroke Play - Two strokes. To avoid a possible infringement, it is better to leave the repair work until completion of the hole.

When your ball is on the putting green, you may remove loose impediments from your line of putt.

Loose impediments may only be removed by using your hand or a club and without pressing down onto the putting green surface. Penalty: Match Play - Loss of hole; Stroke Play - Two strokes.

Sand and loose soil are loose impediments only when they are on the putting green.

You must not remove dew or frost from your line of putt or from the immediate vicinity of your ball, unless this occurs in the act of addressing the ball, when clearing your line of loose impediments or when repairing pitch marks or an old hole plug.

When your ball is on the putting green, if casual water is lying between your ball and the hole, you may take maximum relief by moving the ball until you find the nearest clear line to the hole but the new position of the ball must not be nearer the hole or in a hazard. Whether this new position is on or off the surface of the putting green, the ball must be **placed** not dropped. Penalty: Match Play - Loss of hole; Stroke Play - Two strokes.

Snow and natural ice may be treated as casual water or loose impediments. You have the option of determining which in any given situation. If there is either on your line of putt, take relief as you would for casual water, or remove the ice/snow from your line of putt as you would for loose impediments, provided that the latter does not unduly hold up play.

When you come across an extra hole on or near the putting green, you are entitled to take relief, without penalty, because a hole made by a Greenkeeper is ground under repair. When the ball is on the putting green, if the hole interferes with your line of putt or your stance, lift and place the ball at the **nearest** spot to give you a clear putt to the hole. If this spot is off the surface of the putting green, you must still **place** the ball, not drop it. When the ball is **off** the putting green, if the extra hole interferes with your stroke or stance, lift and drop the ball within one club-length of the NPR, not nearer the hole. You do not get relief without penalty for line of play interference when your ball is off the putting green.

When your ball is on the putting green, your partner, his caddie or your caddie may point out the line of putt to you but this must be done without touching the putting green. Penalty: Match Play - Loss of hole; Stroke Play - Two strokes.

When giving you assistance with your putt, your partner or caddie may stand behind the ball on or near your line of putt but must move away before you putt the ball or you will be penalised: Match Play - Loss of hole; Stroke Play - Two strokes.

When your ball is on the line of another player's putt, you may be asked to mark your ball one or two putterhead-lengths away to one side or the other. When replacing the ball, do not forget to reverse the process or you will be penalised: Match Play - Loss of hole; Stroke Play - Two strokes. However, provided that you become aware of the error before you putt, you may correct it without penalty.

Before playing a stroke on the putting green, you should have any ball which is on or near your line of putt lifted because, if your ball collides with another ball on the green, you will be penalised two strokes in stroke play but there is no penalty in match play. Your ball is then played as it lies and the other player must replace his ball or he will be penalised: Match Play - Loss of hole; Stroke Play - Two strokes.

If there is another player putting his ball, do not putt yours until the other ball has come to rest. Penalty: Match Play - Loss of hole; Stroke Play - Two strokes. However, if it was your turn to play, you would not incur a penalty.

If you fail to mark the position of your ball before lifting or rotating it, you are subject to a one-stroke penalty.

When you mark and lift your ball on the putting green, it may be cleaned.

When putting, you must not stand astride the line of your putt. Penalty: Match Play - Loss of hole; Stroke Play - Two strokes. Because the player in the diagram is aiming to the left of the pin, the stance is correct. If he had been aiming straight at the pin (the dotted line), his stance would contravene the Rule.

It is also against the Rule, when putting, for either foot to touch an extension of your line of putt behind the ball. Penalty: Match Play - Loss of hole; Stroke Play - Two strokes. Watch those tap-ins!

If, after playing a stroke, your ball overhangs the lip of the hole, you are allowed time to walk up to it without any reasonable delay and wait just **ten seconds** to see if the ball will drop into the hole. If, by that time, the ball has not dropped into the hole, the ball is deemed to be at rest. If the ball subsequently drops into the hole, you are deemed to have holed out on your last stroke but you must add a penalty stroke to your score.

In *match play,* when you concede a putt, say so clearly or pick up your opponent's ball and hand it to him. The latter action avoids any doubt that might otherwise arise. You are not allowed to concede a putt in stroke play.

When your ball is on the putting green, always have the flagstick attended or removed because if the ball strikes the flagstick, you will be penalised: Match Play - Loss of hole; Stroke Play - Two strokes and the ball is then played as it lies.

When the flagstick is attended with your authority, if your ball strikes the flagstick, the person attending the flagstick or equipment carried by that person, you incur the penalty: Match Play - Loss of hole; Stroke Play - Two strokes and the ball is played as it lies.

When your ball is off the putting green, you may elect to have the flagstick left in the hole unattended. If your ball touches the flagstick on its way into the hole, there is no penalty.

When you are making a stroke or your ball is in motion, if your fellow competitor or opponent attends/removes the flagstick from the hole without your knowledge or authority, he will be penalised: Match Play - Loss of hole; Stroke Play - Two strokes. In stroke play, if, under such circumstances, your ball touches the flagstick, the unauthorised attendant or equipment being carried by him, you will not incur a penalty. If the ball was played from the surface of the putting green, the stroke is replayed; if not, the ball is played as it lies.

After removing the flagstick from the hole, it should be placed in such a way that it will not interfere with the ensuing putts because if your ball strikes, or is stopped by the flagstick, you will be penalised: Match Play - Loss of hole; Stroke Play - Two strokes and your ball is played as it lies.

A flagstick which has been placed on the surface of the putting green must not be removed by another player from your line of putt whilst your ball is in motion or **he** will be penalised: Match Play - Loss of hole; Stroke Play - Two strokes.

When your ball is resting against an unattended flagstick after being played from off the putting green, if, when the flagstick is removed, the ball drops into the hole, you are deemed to have holed out on your last stroke. If the ball runs away from the hole, it should be replaced on the lip of the hole and putted for a further stroke, without penalty, but if this happens as a result of your playing partner removing the flagstick without your authority, in match play he incurs one penalty stroke; in stroke play, no penalty is incurred by either player and the ball is then replaced against the flagstick and you start again!

Wrong putting green

If your ball comes to rest on a putting green other than the one you are playing, you must play your next stroke from off the putting green with no penalty and you may clean your ball.

To take relief, drop your ball within one club-length of the nearest spot off the green, not nearer the hole.

REFEREES

When a referee is appointed to oversee a match, his decision is final - whether he is right or wrong!

If you disagree with the referee's decision, you are allowed to take the matter up with the Committee but **only** with the referee's agreement.

A referee should not attend the flagstick.

During play, a referee has the authority to declare an area to be ground under repair.

SCORING

Penalty strokes are counted in your score as they take effect, i.e. before you play the next stroke.

If you incur a penalty, you count it immediately and tell the person responsible for marking your card; you do not wait until the end of the hole.

In *stroke play,* you will be disqualified for returning a card showing a score for a hole which is lower than the number of strokes taken at that hole. The disqualification penalty applies even if the competition has closed unless it was for failing to include a penalty which you did not know you had incurred.

SHELTER from the ELEMENTS

When making a stroke at the ball, you are not allowed the comfort of being sheltered from the pouring rain that runs down the back of your neck or the sleet that stings your cheeks and sticks to your spectacles if it involves help from any other person. Penalty: Match Play - Loss of hole; Stroke Play - Two strokes. However, there is no penalty involved for sheltering under, for example, an umbrella when making a stroke at the ball, provided that you hold the umbrella yourself.

When it is raining 'cats and dogs':

In *stroke play,* if the group in front is within range or is still occupying the next tee, you may take refuge in a nearby shelter, but once they are out of range, you must all be ready to resume play. The penalty for discontinuing play without good reason is disqualification.

In *match play,* if you and your opponent agree to take shelter, as soon as one of you decides that the weather is fit to restart, the match must continue because the **agreement** to discontinue no longer exists.

SUSPENSION of PLAY

Once you commence play, you must continue regardless of the weather, other than if you consider there is danger from lightning; you may then suspend play immediately. *Match play* may be discontinued by agreement with your opponent as long as it does not delay the competition. However, as soon as one of you wishes to continue play, the opponent has no option but to agree to do likewise. A refusal means that the **agreement** to discontinue play no longer exists.

If play is suspended while you are in the middle of playing a hole, you may finish the hole provided that your fellow competitor/marker accompanies you. However, if the Committee has made it a Condition of the Competition that, when necessary, players leave the course immediately, they must do so. Penalty: Disqualification.

When the Committee suspends play, you may mark and lift your ball. When you are discontinuing play because of sudden illness, you think there is lightning about or because you are waiting for a ruling by the Committee, you may not mark and lift your ball unless you intend to leave that particular area and fear that the ball may be moved or taken away.

During suspension of play, you are allowed to discuss club selection or anything else that comes under the heading of advice with your fellow competitor or opponent.

Upon resumption of play:
- if you left your ball, you may now lift, clean and replace it or, indeed, use a substitute ball;
- if you marked and lifted the ball, you may clean and

replace the original or use a substitute ball;
if the ball or marker has been moved or is missing, you may place a ball on the original spot. If this spot is indeterminable, **drop** a ball as near as possible to the estimated position, not nearer the hole, but if the ball was on the putting green, you **place** it - not drop it.

When play is suspended at the end of a particular hole, it is resumed on the tee of the next hole whether it is resumed on the same day, on the following day, or whenever, i.e. you do not start again from the first hole.

When the Committee suspends play, you are not allowed to resume play until there is an official announcement. Penalty: Disqualification. However, when the suspension of play is due to lightning, if you think there is still a threat of lightning, the decision to resume play is yours. But, you will be disqualified if you refuse to resume play when the Committee has done all in its power to establish that no further threat of lightning exists.

TEEING GROUND

Before you even step onto the tee, you should be aware of the following:

Artificial devices

The use of certain artificial devices and unusual equipment is prohibited. For example, if you are playing an unfamiliar course and need to know the location of the flag, by all means get out your binoculars **but** make sure that they haven't a range finder attachment or you will be disqualified.

Foreign matter

You will be disqualified if, for example, you apply saliva or chalk to the face of the club in order to influence the movement of the ball or attach any similar foreign matter to the ball in order to change or improve its playing characteristics.

Mixing match and stroke play

Because of some differences in the Rules, match and stroke play must **not** be played concurrently. If you play a match and have a card marked at the same time, neither the score on the card nor the result of the match is acceptable.

The honour

In the absence of a draw sheet, how do you decide the honour on the first tee? Despite the 'custom and practice' at most Golf Clubs, the Rules of Golf state that the honour should be decided by lot; in other words, by the tossing of a coin or by any other method where chance, and not skill, is involved.

The honour on the next and subsequent tees is dependent

upon the scores for the previous hole, e.g. if you take fewer strokes than your fellow competitor or opponent, you have the honour on the next tee. (Net scores in match play and Stableford competitions and gross scores in stroke play.)

Playing out of turn

When you mistakenly play from the teeing ground in the wrong order there is no penalty but, in match play, your opponent is entitled to immediately ask you to replay the stroke in the correct order. If, in stroke play, you and your fellow competitor(s) deliberately play out of turn in order to give one of you an advantage, both you and the other person(s) concerned will be disqualified.

Irregularities of surface

You are allowed to press down uneven ground on the tee **before** you play your stroke; elsewhere, it is recommended that you do so afterwards. You may even 'create' an irregularity on the tee, if you wish.

Practice swings

If you must take a practice swing on the tee, try to avoid taking a divot. If you do, do not replace it. Practice swings on the tees are not favoured by some Golf Clubs so look out for a notice to this effect which will usually be found on the first tee.

Ball falls off the tee peg

If, when you are addressing the ball, it falls off the tee peg, you may re-tee the ball, no penalty, but if you dislodge the ball when making your stroke, you count the stroke and the ball is then played as it lies.

If you discontinue your swing before the clubhead reaches

the ball, even if the ball falls off the tee peg, you will not be charged a stroke, nor incur a penalty, because you have not made a stroke at the ball.

If you have an air shot on the tee, your ball is now in play. So, when addressing the ball again, if you accidentally touch the ball and it falls off the tee peg, you incur one penalty stroke and the ball must be replaced or the penalty changes to: Match Play - Loss of hole; Stroke Play - Two strokes.

If you have an air shot on the tee, your ball is in play - so don't be tempted to raise or lower your tee peg before the next stroke or you will be penalised one stroke for moving a ball in play and you must replace the ball by repositioning the tee peg to its original position. If you don't, instead of the one stroke penalty, your penalty is now: Match Play - Loss of hole; Stroke Play - Two strokes.

Tee markers

Do not tee your ball in front of the tee markers. The teeing ground is formed by the line between the outer front edge of the markers and an area of up to two club-lengths back behind that line. You may tee up anywhere within the teeing area and stand anywhere, either inside or outside that area, to play your stroke. The tee markers are fixed before you put your ball into play and you will be penalised: Match Play - Loss of hole; Stroke Play - Two strokes if you remove one to facilitate your stroke. Once the ball is in play, the markers become movable obstructions for the remainder of play.

Stroke Play - If you play your ball from outside the teeing ground, you must play again from inside it and add two penalty strokes to your score. (You do not count the stroke(s) played from outside the teeing ground.) The

Teeing Ground

mistake must be rectified before teeing off on the next hole or, if you are on the final hole of the round, a declaration of intent to rectify must be made before leaving the putting green, otherwise the penalty is disqualification.

Match Play: If you play your tee shot from outside the teeing ground, there is no penalty, but your opponent may immediately ask you to replay the stroke from within the teeing ground.

THROUGH the GREEN

'Through the green' is perhaps a confusing definition and newcomers to the game can be forgiven for thinking that it means 'beyond the green' or 'over the green'. In fact, it means the whole area of the course except the teeing ground and putting green of the hole being played and all the bunkers and water/lateral water hazards on the course. This table highlights the areas of a hole which are 'through the green'.

	Through the green
Tee of the hole being played	-
Fairway	Yes
Semi-rough	Yes
Rough	Yes
Bunkers	-
Water/lateral water hazards	-
Green of the hole being played	-
Tee and green of the other holes on the course	Yes

Where 'through the green' is concerned, there is no difference in status between the fairway and the rough.

UNPLAYABLE BALL

You may deem your ball unplayable anywhere on the course **except** when it is in a water/lateral water hazard.

There are three courses of action open to you when you inform your fellow competitor, opponent or marker that you are deeming your ball unplayable. You may:
- take a stroke-and-distance penalty which means going back to where you played the last stroke, forfeiting distance and adding a penalty stroke to your score; or
- implement the 'Go back as far as you like' (GBL) procedure, which also involves adding a penalty stroke to your score; or
- drop a ball within two club-lengths of the spot where your ball lay, not nearer the hole, and adding a penalty stroke to your score.

When you deem your ball unplayable in a bunker, you may:
- take a stroke-and-distance penalty; or
- implement the GBL procedure but the ball must be dropped in the bunker for a penalty stroke; or
- drop your ball in the bunker within two club-lengths of where the ball lay, not nearer the hole, for a penalty stroke.

To implement the 'Go back as far as you like' procedure:
Draw an imaginary line from the hole to a spot on which you wish to drop the ball, keeping the position of where the ball lay between these two points.

WATER/LATERAL WATER HAZARDS

A water hazard is a pond, ditch, stream or the like, whether or not it contains water. It should be defined by yellow lines and/or stakes. Both the lines and the stakes are part of the hazard.

A water hazard, or part of a water hazard, may be deemed to be a lateral water hazard by the Committee if it is **impracticable** to drop a ball in accordance with the GBL procedure; it should then be marked with red lines and/or stakes.

A water/lateral water hazard extends from the uppermost part of the bank on the one side of the hazard to the uppermost part of the bank on the other side of the hazard. It also extends vertically downwards and upwards to infinity, a point to remember if your ball is lodged in a tree or bush within a water/lateral water hazard.

Whether your ball is 2" or 20" below the margin of a hazard, regardless of whether it contains any water, when you play the ball as it lies you must **not** ground the club or remove or touch a loose impediment before you play your stroke. Penalty: Match Play - Loss of hole; Stroke Play - Two strokes. A stroke is the forward movement of the club and does not include your backswing.

You may **not** declare your ball unplayable in a water/lateral water hazard.

When your ball lies in a water/lateral water hazard, there is no penalty for touching the ground or water in the hazard with your club before playing your stroke when:
- removing an obstruction;
- probing for your ball;
- retrieving the ball; or
- preventing a fall or as a result of a fall;

providing you do not test the condition of the hazard or improve the lie of your ball, the penalty for which is: Match Play - Loss of hole; Stroke Play   Two strokes.

When your ball is in a **water hazard** you have three options:
(1)   play the ball as it lies
(2)   take a stroke-and-distance penalty
(3)   implement the GBL procedure, for one penalty stroke, keeping the point where the ball last crossed the margin of the hazard between the hole and where you drop your ball.

When your ball is in a **lateral water hazard** you have the additional option:
(4)   of taking a two club-length penalty drop measured either from the point where the ball last crossed the margin of the hazard, or, on the opposite margin, if practical, equidistant from the hole.

If you opt for (2), (3) or (4), you may clean your ball or use a substitute ball.

To show you what is meant by equidistant from the hole, I have drawn one line (A) from the hole to the point where the ball last crossed the margin of the hazard and another line (B) from the hole to the opposite margin, both lines being of equal length. As you will see, the point equidistant from the hole on the opposite margin is not directly opposite the point where the ball crossed the margin of the hazard.

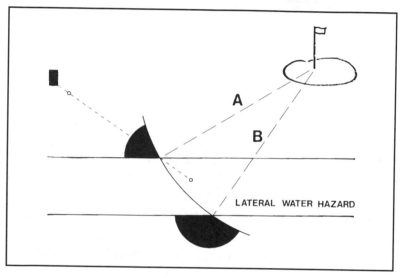

NOTE 1   The shaded parts indicate the area in which you are allowed to measure and drop your ball within two club-lengths.

NOTE 2   Provided that the opposite margin of the bank is not out of bounds, to implement the GBL procedure, the imaginary line will be on an extension of line A.

When you need to mark and lift your ball from a water/lateral water hazard, if the lie of the ball has been altered, replace the ball in the hazard in a similar lie which is not nearer the hole but is as near as possible to, but not more than one

---

        Water/Lateral Water Hazards

club-length away from, the original lie of the ball.

When you are playing your ball as it lies in the water, there is no penalty for playing a moving ball, i.e. if the flow of the water is moving the ball.

When your ball lies on a bridge spanning a water/lateral water hazard, you are allowed to ground your club and touch the bridge on your backswing; the bridge is an obstruction and there is no penalty for touching an obstruction in a hazard. This also applies if the bridge is an integral part of the course.

While playing your ball from within a water/lateral water hazard, if you fail to get it out of the hazard, your options are the same as (1), (2), (3) and (4) but with the additional option (5), also for a penalty stroke, of playing the ball again from where the last stroke was played outside the hazard. Remember, when taking option (2), you will still be playing from within the hazard and, of course, there is no penalty for taking option (1). However, if, after dropping your ball under option (2), it comes to rest in a place from which, in your opinion, you cannot play, you may take option (3) or (5) counting one penalty stroke for dropping your ball under option (2) and one penalty stroke for taking option (3) or (5).

If, after playing your ball from within the hazard, it goes out of bounds, is lost or comes to rest in an unplayable lie outside the hazard, you may take option (2) for one penalty stroke; option (3) or (4) for two penalty strokes but the reference point is where the ball crossed the margin when it went into the hazard; or option (5) for two penalty strokes. However, if, after dropping your ball under option (2) you decide not to play it, you may still take option (3), (4) or (5).

When your ball crosses the margin of the hazard twice, the reference point you use for the GBL procedure is where the ball last crossed the margin of the hazard. In this diagram, the straight line shows the path of the ball and the reference point (X) is where the ball last crossed the margin

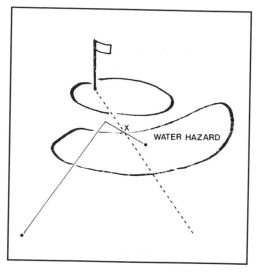

of the hazard. The dotted line is the imaginary line you use for the GBL procedure.

If you play your ball into a stream and the flow of the water takes it out of bounds, your ball is out of bounds and you must take a stroke-and-distance penalty.

If your ball goes into a stream which is out of bounds and the flow of the water brings it back into bounds, the ball is in bounds. If the ball is now in a water hazard, you may play the ball as it lies, implement the 'Go back as far as you like' (GBL) procedure or take a stroke-and-distance penalty.

To implement the GBL procedure, the reference point you keep between the hole and where you drop the ball is where the ball re-entered the course at the boundary line. If, due to the nature of the course, you find it impossible to drop behind the hazard on a line from the hole through this reference point, you are allowed to treat the water hazard as a lateral water hazard and take a two club-length penalty drop on either side of the hazard, equidistant from the hole. Diagram on page 120. The ball when dropped must not come to rest nearer the hole.

When playing a ball from within a water/lateral water hazard, if either your stance or the area of your intended swing is impeded by an immovable obstruction, e.g. an exposed pipe, a wall, a bridge, etc, you are not allowed relief without penalty. The normal options for a ball in a water/lateral water hazard apply.

Your ball is lost in a water/lateral water hazard only when there is reasonable evidence that your ball entered the hazard.

There is no 'free' relief from casual water, ground under repair, a burrowing animal hole or an immovable obstruction in a water/lateral water hazard.

WRONG BALL

The strokes played with the wrong ball are not counted in the score and neither is there a penalty for playing the wrong ball out of a hazard whether it be a bunker or a water/lateral water hazard.

The penalty for playing the wrong ball, except from a hazard is: Match Play - Loss of hole; Stroke Play - Two strokes. In stroke play, the mistake must be rectified before teeing off on the next hole, or, if you are on the final hole of the round, a declaration of intent to rectify must be made before leaving the putting green, otherwise you will be disqualified.

Even if you hole out before realising that you have inadvertently played the wrong ball, the error must be rectified, as above.

In *stroke play,* if you are not able to establish where the wrong ball was played, you will be disqualified, because, without knowing this, it is impossible to rectify the error.

In *match play,* if you and your opponent discover that you have exchanged balls, the one who played the wrong ball first (other than from a hazard) loses the hole. If you are not able to decide who played the wrong ball first, play on with the balls exchanged until you both hole out.

If your fellow competitor or opponent mistakenly plays your ball which comes to rest some distance away, you may substitute that ball by **placing** another one on the original spot. If this spot is indeterminable, **drop** a ball (if on the putting green, place the ball) as near as possible to the original position. Be sure to tell your fellow competitor, opponent or marker the name and number of the substituted ball.

NOTE You should always play the same ball if it is immediately recoverable, i.e. if it can be retrieved without holding up play.

In a *four-ball match play* competition, if your partner plays a wrong ball, except from a hazard, he will be disqualified from playing out the remainder of the hole but you will not be penalised even if the ball belongs to you.

You are allowed five minutes to search for your ball but, in *stroke play,* if you play a wrong ball inside the five minute limit, the time spent playing that ball does not count against the search time. In *match play*, as soon as you play a wrong ball, you lose the hole!

WRONG PLACE - Playing from

Playing from outside the teeing area or from the wrong tee
Stroke play: If you play your tee shot from outside the teeing ground, you must play again from inside it and add two penalty strokes to your score. (You do not count the stroke(s) played from outside the teeing ground.) The mistake must be rectified before teeing off on the next hole or, if you are on the final hole of the round, a declaration of intent to rectify must be made before leaving the putting green, otherwise the penalty is disqualification.

Match play: If you play your tee shot from outside the teeing ground there is no penalty, but your opponent may immediately ask you to replay the stroke from within the teeing ground.

Playing from wrong place other than the teeing ground or wrong teeing ground
Match play: When taking relief, if you drop or place your ball in a wrong place and play it from the wrong place, you will lose the hole.

Stroke play
When taking relief, if you drop or place your ball in a wrong place, and play it from the wrong place, you will be penalised under that rule. For clarification:

Example 1
Your ball is in a lateral water hazard and when taking the two club-length penalty drop, you drop your ball slightly nearer the hole than where it last crossed the margin of the hazard. When you play this ball you are playing from a wrong place so you are penalised two strokes for infringement of the

lateral water hazard rule and you must play out the hole with this ball. BUT, if you had dropped the ball, say, a significant distance nearer the hole, this would be a serious breach of the rule for which you will be disqualified unless you correct the error as follows:

To correct error after serious breach
Tell your playing partner that you will play a second ball from the correct place and play out the hole with the two balls. You must do this before teeing off on the next hole, or, if on the last hole of the round, you must declare your intention to rectify before leaving the putting green. After you have finished play and before signing your card, you must report the matter to the Committee. If they decide that it was a serious breach, the score with the second ball will be accepted with a two stroke penalty.

Example 2
You cannot find your ball and you drop and play another ball from where the original ball is lost instead of taking a stroke-and-distance penalty. Penalty: Two strokes for infringing the rule as well as one stroke for the stroke-and-distance penalty you should have taken, and you play out the hole with this ball. But, if this is a serious breach, you must take a stroke-and-distance penalty with a second ball and correct as shown in Example 1.

Example 3
You play your ball, it hits a tractor (an outside agency) and goes out of bounds. In your ignorance, you drop and play another ball from a spot near to where the ball hit the tractor. But, as your ball is out of bounds, the correct procedure is to take a stroke-and-distance penalty. By playing from the tractor you were playing from nearer the hole than if you had

played from where you played the last stroke. If this is a serious breach of the rule you will be disqualified if you do not play a second ball by taking the stroke-and-distance penalty and proceed as shown in Example 1.

Example 4
You play your ball towards an area of GUR and if you fail to find it, you may not assume that it is lost in the GUR and expect to take a free drop. You must have reasonable evidence that your ball entered the GUR in order to assume that it is lost in the GUR. Without this reasonable evidence, if you drop your ball outside the GUR instead of taking a stroke-and-distance penalty, you will be penalised two strokes for infringing this rule as well as the one stroke for the stroke-and-distance penalty you should have taken and play out the hole with this ball. If you think this is a serious breach, you must now take a stroke-and-distance penalty with a second ball and proceed as shown in Example 1.

Wrong Place - Playing from

NOTES